THE ESSENTIAL GUIDE TO
HIKING
WITH DOGS

FALCON®

An imprint of The Rowman & Littlefield Publishing Group, Inc.
4501 Forbes Blvd., Ste. 200
Lanham, MD 20706
www.rowman.com
Falcon and FalconGuides are registered trademarks and Make Adventure Your Story is a trademark
of The Rowman & Littlefield Publishing Group, Inc.

Distributed by NATIONAL BOOK NETWORK

British Library Cataloguing in Publication Information available

Library of Congress Cataloging-in-Publication Data

Names: Sotolongo, Jen, 1982– author.
Title: The essential guide to hiking with dogs : trail-tested tips and expert advice for canine
    adventures / Jen Sotolongo.
Description: Guilford, Connecticut : Falcon, [2021] | "Distributed by NATIONAL BOOK
    NETWORK"— T.p. verso. | Summary: "Need-to-know topics for novice hikers or new owners,
    from trail etiquette to leave no trace ethics, important gear and packing guides to essential
    commands you should train on the trail. Color photography throughout"— Provided by
    publisher.
Identifiers: LCCN 2020052110 (print) | LCCN 2020052111 (ebook) | ISBN 9781493055968
    (paperback : acid-free paper) | ISBN 9781493055975 (ePub)
Subjects: LCSH: Hiking with dogs—Guidebooks.
Classification: LCC SF427.455 .S68 2021 (print) | LCC SF427.455 (ebook) | DDC 796.51—dc23
LC record available at https://lccn.loc.gov/2020052110
LC ebook record available at https://lccn.loc.gov/2020052111

∞™ The paper used in this publication meets the minimum requirements of American National
Standard for Information Sciences—Permanence of Paper for Printed Library Materials, ANSI/
NISO Z39.48-1992.

THE ESSENTIAL GUIDE TO
HIKING
WITH DOGS

Trail-Tested Tips and Expert Advice for Canine Adventures

JEN SOTOLONGO

FALCON®

Guilford, Connecticut

CONTENTS

INTRODUCTION

AS A CHILD, I HAD ALWAYS WANTED A DOG. My parents didn't want to take on the responsibility, so to get my dog fix, I became the neighborhood dog walker and pet sitter. I made friends with anyone who had a dog. For an introverted kid, dogs were my ticket to confidence, practicing talking to people I didn't know.

Finally, in the winter of 2012, in the first year of my 30s, I began a relationship with someone who came with two dogs: Maxwell, an older rat terrier, and Sora, a beautiful blue merle Australian shepherd.

I instantly fell head over heels for Sora and, despite a fear of new people, she also took to me right away. I did everything wrong when I met her. You see, I was one of those people who used to believe that dogs love me because I love them. I took Sora's face in my hands and machine-washed her head as my introduction. I'm very lucky that she didn't bite me.

I thought I knew a lot about dogs from my days as the neighborhood dog sitter. Sora, however, taught me to forget everything I thought I knew. Rescued at three years old, Sora was nervous around new people, did not like children, and was reactive to other dogs. She didn't appreciate when strangers petted her on the head or bent down into her face (as I've since learned, most dogs do not actually enjoy this).

I learned to cross the street if we saw others walking toward us. Hiking with her was stressful. I learned the hard way that she had not earned off-leash rights, and I fretted constantly about strange off-leash dogs approaching us on the trail. I learned to speak dog, read dog body language, and advocate for her on her behalf. Most importantly, I learned that not all dogs love me just because I love them.

Sora's challenges shaped me into the knowledgeable dog owner I am today.

From 2015 to 2017, Sora joined us for a two-year bicycle tour across Europe and South America, an adventure that took us to twenty-four countries. Since we spent a lot of time on our bicycles, when we returned home to the Pacific Northwest, I was eager to get back on the trails.

Returning to my home state of Washington as an avid outdoorswoman in my adulthood, I took the opportunity to explore the trails in my own state and brought Sora along for every mile.

Before Sora entered my life, I spent many hours alone running on trails. Although there is really very little difference between trail running and hiking, walking alone on a trail in

the woods felt more daunting. Sora gave me the confidence to face that fear, and soon we hit the trails as a duo regularly.

Throughout the summer, we ticked off trail after trail. As the longer days waned, I discovered the striking fall colors in the North Cascades and Snoqualmie Alps. Come winter, we escaped the rain and went to higher elevations in search of snow. By spring, we could hardly wait for the array of wildflowers that would sprout once the snow melted.

She also helped me develop friendships with fellow dog adventurers all over the world.

I had started a blog called Long Haul Trekkers when we left for our bike trip, which told the stories of our adventures on two wheels. That blog eventually evolved into a source for adventure dogs, offering information about getting outside with your dog. I developed my photography skills and grew our online presence, particularly on Instagram.

Usually a bit of a Luddite, I had never taken to social media; however, I wanted to share Sora's story, and in the process I created a community with fellow adventure dogs and their humans all over the world. We met Tala and Jura in Ecuador; Sora became the voice of adoption for a rescue organization during an extended stay in Medellin, Colombia; and fellow cyclists Didier and Kyla spotted our telltale dog trailer while battling the brutal Patagonian winds and pulled over just to meet Sora.

When we departed on our bike trip, we noticed a small black growth on Sora's right paw. Our vet waved it off as a corn and we thought nothing of it until it began to grow, and eventually bleed. A biopsy in Berlin confirmed our worst nightmare: cancer. A nerve sheath tumor with a propensity to return.

For three years, Sora battled this cancer. The lump would return, we'd have it surgically removed, including twice during our bicycle trip, and hoped that would be the end of it. Unfortunately, each time the tumor grew back, it did so with a vengeance, becoming more and more difficult to fully remove, thanks to the medusa-like roots that intertwined with her muscles and tissue. Eventually, we chose to resort to cancer treatments, including electrochemotherapy and radiation therapy. Neither worked.

Sora never fully recovered from her last treatment, but she continued to join us on the trails. I massaged CBD oil onto her leg, the skin now fully exposed from the radiation therapy, wrapped her damaged skin in bandages, and we'd set off in the mountains. During her last summer, we took a road trip throughout Europe, meeting friends old and new, continuing to show her the world.

Days after returning from that trip, she stopped eating. For a dog that would knock down a wall for a nibble of food, I knew this sign indicated the end of our adventure together. A few weeks later, when her oncologist told us she had something in her lungs that was pushing on her diaphragm, making it painful to eat, we knew what we had to do.

We took Sora for one last adventure.

Too weak to hike from the lack of eating, we set off to the beach and arose early for short sunrise walks. We paddleboarded in the Mediterranean Sea and sat with her on the patio while she basked in the sun.

Days after our return, we made the most heartbreakingly painful decision of our lives and gave Sora one final gift: freedom from cancer and pain.

Today, I am back in the Pacific Northwest, exploring the trails with my adopted cattle dog, Sitka. Like Sora, he comes with his own set of challenges, and together we work through them, building our bond and establishing our roles as an adventure team, ticking off hike after hike.

HANNAH ZULUETA

WHO IS THIS BOOK FOR?

THIS BOOK IS FOR ADVENTURE DOGS AND THEIR PEOPLE.

It is especially for those who used to be the dog owner I once was, the dog owner many of us once were. These are the dog owners who love to take their dogs along on the trails, who love their dogs more than anything, but who don't understand dog behavior and how it impacts the trail experience.

I have made many mistakes with my dogs. I have allowed them to run off leash with abandon, believing they could only have a good time when let loose and free, resulting in unwanted and embarrassing interactions with other trail users.

Since I rescue and love herding dogs, my dogs are typically reactive to other dogs and sometimes people. I so badly wanted my dogs to be that off-leash dog that would come to me when called and walk by my side, but I didn't understand the amount of training and dedication involved to make that happen.

The most humiliating encounter I ever had occurred 16 miles into an 18-mile trail run, when Sora and I came upon a group of senior bird-watchers. Two of them had dogs, and Sora was off leash on a leash-required trail. I was tired and out of treats and therefore not of value to Sora.

She went straight up to the first dog and lunged at him, causing him to yelp, which sent an echo of horrified shrieks down the line of birders. She did the same with the second dog. A man at the end of the line tried to corral her for me, and I had to practically leap to the ground in front of him to stop him from approaching her.

Never again did I allow Sora off leash where I didn't deem it safe for her, and for all other users.

I am the dog owner I am today because of the mistakes I have made with my dogs. We will all make them at some point, and my hope with this book is that I can show you how to be an exemplary trail user with your dog in order to avoid uncomfortable and potentially dangerous situations for you, your dog, and others in the outdoors.

I also want you to have fun with your dog. I have met so many people who became avid hikers, all thanks to their dogs. My goal is to teach you about dog behavior, provide training advice, and incorporate etiquette suggestions so that you and your dog can share a lifetime of outdoor adventure together.

With that said, I want to make it very clear that I am not a dog trainer, nor a dog behaviorist. I am not a dog nutritionist, and I have no veterinary background. I am a dog mom who has been blogging and writing about dogs for many years. My journalism background and my passion and interest in the subject matter mean that I spend a lot of time researching and asking questions of qualified individuals. I have provided the information in this book to the best of my ability, based on what I have learned and studied from professionals and other highly knowledgeable individuals.

CHAPTER 1

FINDING THE RIGHT ADVENTURE BUDDY

I SHOULDN'T HAVE SITKA, THE DOG I HAVE NOW. After a fall relationship breakup left me dogless, I borrowed friends' dogs for hikes and runs while I searched for my own. With an out-of-town winter holiday cat-sitting gig, I knew I'd have to wait until after the holidays to find my next best friend.

Of course, that didn't stop me from perusing adoption sites online in the meantime. I was looking for a very specific dog and I knew it would take awhile to find. As a way of putting my search out into the Universe, I announced what I was looking for on my Instagram feed: an Australian shepherd or cattle dog *with* a tail.

In November I found the profile for Dakota, now Sitka, and saved it, knowing that I'd likely never meet him.

But then an Instagram friend sent me his profile and offered to go meet him since she lived in the same small town. I hesitated, but when another friend also sent me his profile, I obliged. "Yes, please go meet him," I said to the friend whom I only knew through photos and comments on a social media app.

She did, and hesitated to tell me how much she adored him, since she knew I couldn't get him until after Christmas.

On my way down to my cat-sitting job in Bend, Oregon, I made an appointment to meet Sitka. Moments after walking into the backyard to meet him, he tore a small tooth mark puncture into my jacket. I knew right then and there that he would be mine. If I had puncture marks in my favorite coat, it was going to be from my own dog.

Of course I fell for him, but I had to figure out what to do with nearly a month before I could take him home. I again put it out to the Universe to see if he was really meant to be mine.

Thanksgiving came and went and nobody came to claim him. Then, another Instagram friend, another whom I had never met, offered to foster him for the remaining time until I could pick him up on Christmas Eve and take him back home with me to Seattle.

Most dog owners will tell you that story of the moment they knew they had found the right dog; often the story goes that the dog selected them. No matter how the story happens, that first day is just the beginning of many wonderful years ahead.

SO YOU GOT A NEW PUPPY!

How very exciting! Congratulations on the new member of your pack. My hope is that this book will guide you through the steps toward shaping your new puppy into a wonderful adventure buddy.

The hardest part for me about having a puppy isn't all the potty training and enduring razor-sharp teeth meeting my skin on a daily basis, it's (not so) patiently awaiting the day it can join me on the trail.

Puppies have seemingly endless energy, and many falsely believe that the only way to tire out a puppy is to let it run all day long. This is a common misconception among dog owners and can result in long-term effects down the line.

While the research and opinions are varied, most sources will say that puppies should partake in limited "forced exercise" activities until their growth plates have finished growing. Forced exercise simply means anything dictated by the human and on leash, such as going on a 5-mile hike because that is the length of the hike, as opposed to a beach trip where your puppy can run free and rest when it feels tired.

Many veterinarians will agree that allowing your puppy to engage in too much forced exercise before its growth plates have finished growing can result in a number of osteo problems, including hip dysplasia and arthritis.

The general guideline states that puppies should have 5 minutes of exercise per month of age, no more than twice daily. For example, a six-month-old puppy can go for two 30-minute walks or easy hikes per day.

Other medical professionals will argue that it depends on the dog and your lifestyle and suggest using common sense. Learn the signs of fatigue and base your adventures according to their abilities.

The bottom line is that there is no strict recipe when it comes to hiking and dogs. Larger dogs take longer for their bones to complete growth than smaller dogs. The average length of time before a puppy has full clearance to exercise ranges between twelve and eighteen months, depending on the breed and size.

Either way, too much too soon is asking for injury. Regular hikers or runners may be able to increase average weekly mileage in their puppies sooner than weekend warriors, simply because their dogs will have that base.

ADOPTING VS. BUYING FROM A BREEDER

If you had asked me even just a few years ago, I would have told you that buying a dog from a breeder is irresponsible and contributes to shelter animal deaths. Like many beliefs I once held about dog ownership, this is one where I have unlearned the assumptions I was taught to believe and instead began to listen to those who have chosen to get their dogs from responsible breeders.

While I personally will likely always adopt any new companions from a shelter, there is nothing wrong with others choosing to buy a dog from a breeder. Neither option is "good" or "bad." What is most important is that the dog lives in a good home.

Regardless of where you choose to get your dog, understanding the options and process for both will ensure that you find the right dog for you.

ADOPTING

If you're not picky about the breed of dog you want, are looking for an adolescent or adult dog, and want a dog sooner rather than later, then you'll have no trouble finding a dog in a local shelter or online.

A common misconception is that shelter dogs were all abused or have behavioral issues. Dogs are surrendered for a number of reasons, including divorce, moving, lack of time, and more. You can find a great companion from a shelter.

Local Shelters

Your first instinct might be to look for pets at your local shelters. Here you can see the dogs in person and meet them. Most will allow you to take the dogs out to spend one-on-one time together, and introduce them to your other dog if you have one already.

This gives you the opportunity to get an idea of the dog's demeanor and personality, but keep in mind that life in a shelter is very different from life at your home. The dog may behave differently once in a new place.

If you are looking for a specific breed, then expect to wait awhile before your pup arrives at the shelter. Dogs come and go constantly and they have no idea what they will get from week to week. Let the staff know exactly what you are looking for and ask them to call you if that dog arrives.

Foster Homes

Often, shelters and rescue organizations will send dogs to foster homes to live instead of staying at the shelter. Sometimes they do this because there is no space in the shelter, because the dog has special needs, or for any number of other reasons.

Getting a dog that has been in a foster home will give you a better idea of how it behaves in a house, possibly even with other animals, if the foster home has pets. They can tell you more information about the dog, and if they are an especially great foster home, they will start working on obedience skills with it.

You can visit their home, take your potential new friend for a walk, and ask the foster parents very specific questions.

I got Sitka from a foster situation, and I spent about an hour with him. I asked a friend to bring her dog so we could see how he does with other dogs, and the foster parent kindly brought him to a veterinary office to see how he did with cats.

The Internet

These days, you can find dogs to adopt from across the country and even the world, thanks to the World Wide Web. There are many sites available that will allow you to search by breed, age, size, and more. You can save dogs you like and set up notifications to alert you when the dog of your dreams appears.

If you are willing to drive the distance or pay to have a dog transferred to your state, then your search widens exponentially. If you are searching for a very specific dog, you're sure to find it on the many pet-finding websites.

Breed-Specific Rescue Groups

For those looking for specific breeds or even classes of dogs (i.e., Australian shepherd vs. herding dogs), breed-specific rescue groups are the way to go. They specialize in that specific dog or class of dog and will more likely have the ideal dog for you at some point.

These are very popular and dogs adopt out quickly, so make yourself known to these groups and ask them to keep an eye out for you if you're looking for a specific dog.

Facebook Groups

Breed-specific Facebook groups, local dog groups, or hiking groups will occasionally post about dogs needing to be rehomed. Join a few groups, introduce yourself, engage, and let the group members know what you're looking for. You never know who knows what, and they might just know where your new pal might be.

Adoption pros:

> It's more affordable.

> You could be saving a life.

> It's easier to find a fully grown dog.

> You can find a mutt.

> You can take home a dog that day.

Adoption cons:

> You don't really know what you're going to get.

> It can take a long time to find the right dog if you are looking for something specific.

> The health and history of the dog is unknown.

> › It can be more difficult to find puppies.

> › Dogs may require more training to unlearn old undesirable behaviors.

BUYING FROM A RESPONSIBLE BREEDER

If you decide to get your dog from a breeder, you will want to do a lot of homework to ensure that you have selected a responsible breeder. Here are some tips for finding a trustworthy breeder.

Meet the Breeder and View the Facility

You'll know within minutes if a breeder is running a clean operation during a visit. The facilities will be spotless and puppies will appear healthy, clean, and well fed. They won't be crowded in cages and they'll have space to roam. The puppies and the parents should be outgoing with strangers.

During your visit, you should ask to meet the parents. This will give you some idea of what you can expect from a puppy in terms of temperament, size, and appearance.

A good breeder will be there for your dog throughout its life. If, for whatever reason, you need to give your dog up, a responsible breeder will take the dog back.

Ask the Right Questions

Since the breeder knows your potential pup and its parents better than you ever will, he or she should be able to answer your questions easily and without hesitation. You can never ask too many questions. Breeders want their dogs to go to good homes and will welcome any and all inquiries.

Take note of how the breeder responds: Are they patient and do they have the answers to the majority of your questions off hand? If not, have they promised to look up the answer and get back to you?

Here are a few sample questions to ask:

> › What is your breeding history and experience with the breed?

> › What health tests have been performed on the parents to ensure they have no genetic diseases associated with the breed?

> › How do you socialize the puppies?

> › Have you turned down a sale before? (The answer should be yes, which indicates that they don't allow their puppies to go home to just anyone.)

> Are the puppies up-to-date with their vaccinations?

> Are the dogs members of the AKC or another breeding club?

> Do you provide a health guarantee and contract?

> When will I be able to take the puppy home?

> What requirements do you seek in those looking to buy a puppy?

> Are you as breeders involved with any local agility, tracking, performance, or obedience clubs?

> Do you sell your dogs to pet stores, online, or to brokers? (The answer should be no.)

Prepare for Questions from the Breeder

A quality breeder will actively seek out the right home for their puppies and won't sell them to people on the spot. Many will take reservations for future litters once they have evaluated that you are a good fit.

Be prepared to answer a few questions and provide documentation in certain cases. Breeders may ask or require:

> Why you want a dog and why this specific breed.

> They will ask about your experience with dogs and with the breed.

> If you live in an apartment, rental home, or condo, they may request written confirmation from your landlord as proof that you are able to have a dog.

> They may ask about the rules you will require of the dog at home and where the dog will spend most of its time.

> If you have had other pets, they may request a veterinary reference.

> They may require that you sign a contract indicating that you will spay or neuter your dog, provided you don't plan to breed or show it.

Ask for Referrals

Ask your breeder to provide references of other families who have purchased dogs from them. You can talk candidly with these families to get a better sense of what to expect when you get a dog from this particular breeder.

Breeder pros:

> You will have a better idea of your dog's temperament.

> You can get exactly what you are looking for in terms of appearance, coloration, and breed.

> You have the medical history of the parents.

Breeder cons:

> It can be tough to find the right breeder.

> You may have to wait years before you get your dog.

> Purebred dogs are pricey.

> Breeders can be selective about who their dogs go to (which is a good thing).

PLACES TO AVOID SEARCHING FOR A DOG

Whether you get a dog from a breeder or from a rescue, keep an eye out for red flags. Both routes include irresponsible methods, so it's important to know the signs and stay far away.

BACKYARD BREEDERS (BYBS): Backyard breeders are dog breeders with little knowledge or experience of breeding dogs. They don't generally know the medical and genetic history of the parents and therefore do not selectively breed to avoid common diseases. Dogs are not registered with any kennel or breed clubs.

PUPPY MILLS: Puppy mills are large-scale breeding operations. Think of them like factory farms that value profit over the well-being of the dog. The puppies are housed in unsanitary conditions and are not healthy or well fed.

They call themselves kennels and breeders, so it's easy to be misled. If your prospective breeder cannot provide any of the requests listed above, there's a good chance something fishy is going on and you should look for another breeder.

DOG FLIPPERS: Most common in the Midwest, dog flipping is a terrible business that involves stealing a dog and then selling it on a website like Craigslist for a reasonable fee. This tricks buyers into believing they are getting a purebred dog for a steal (pun intended).

If you suspect a dog you find online has been flipped, check local Facebook groups for reports of missing dogs.

PET STORES (BUT NOT ALWAYS): Puppy mill dogs often end up in pet stores. The caveat is when a pet store runs a local adoption drive or hosts dogs from a legitimate rescue group. There will be representatives from the group at the store or there will be information available if the store is acting as a foster for the pet.

CRAIGSLIST AND OTHER SIMILAR SITES (BUT NOT ALWAYS): Accidental pregnancies, common in more rural areas, are not all that uncommon. The result is unwanted puppies, and these can be found on sites like Craigslist. If you don't mind getting a dog with an unknown genetic history, then you can take a chance. The owner should charge a nominal fee, mostly to weed out people wanting a free dog.

HOW TO PICK THE RIGHT DOG FOR YOU

It's too easy to fall for a cute face, certain breed, or beautiful fur pattern when you go in search of your new adventure buddy, but don't let your emotions take over the practical side. This is a ten- to twenty-year commitment, and you need to be sure that this is the right dog for you and your family.

WHAT BREED DO YOU WANT?

If you want a dog, there's a good chance that you have a breed or two in mind. Maybe it was the same breed your family had growing up, or perhaps your friend has a dog of this breed that you adore. If you are inexperienced with the breed, then make sure you do your research to understand the dog's needs.

Don't get a border collie if you work all day and can only take it out on the weekends for short runs. Don't get a Great Dane if you run ultramarathons. Are you willing to secure your yard if you choose a husky (who are notorious escape artists)? Pick a breed that matches your lifestyle and know exactly what you're getting into if you want that breed.

PUPPY VS. FULLY GROWN DOG

Puppies are adorable. They're also a lot of work. If you are not up to the task, then opt for a fully grown dog. I've adopted puppies and I've adopted 8-year-old dogs. Age doesn't always mean less work, but rather different work, depending on the past life of the dog.

With a puppy, you are in the position to shape that dog from the start of its life, especially during that crucial impression phase of its life. However, getting an older dog doesn't mean that you can't shape it to behave how you envision, it just may take more work.

Also remember that if you choose a puppy, you will have to wait several months and sometimes well over a year before it can join you for proper hike.

WHAT SIZE DOG IS IDEAL?

This is totally up to your own preferences. Small dogs can be just as tough as larger dogs. I personally like to base the size on whether I can carry them down a mountain in an emergency or help them move around as they age.

Apartment dwellers often face size restrictions, which I personally believe is unfair, but, alas, I do not make the rules. The erroneous thought is that larger dogs can be more destructive, don't do well in apartments, and a whole long list of assumptions that are not necessarily true.

Large dogs can do just fine in apartments, provided they get their daily required physical and mental stimulation. Dogs can't get their daily exercise in a yard, anyway.

ARE YOU A CASUAL HIKER OR ENDURANCE FIEND?

If you train for ultramarathons or dream of thru-hiking with your four-legged pal by your side, then look for dogs bred for endurance. Herders, hunting dogs, and retrievers all make great long-distance pals.

The aforementioned breeds are not exclusively ideal for longer endurance feats. I know of plenty of small dogs that join their humans for long runs. But some are naturally better suited to specific sports over others.

Casual hikers should look for lower-energy breeds that are happy to hang out at home most days and then go for an adventure once or twice per week. Consider lower-maintenance breeds like greyhounds, terriers, and some spaniels.

ARE YOU WILLING TO REHABILITATE A DOG WITH BEHAVIORAL ISSUES?

It's easy to say, "Oh yes! I solemnly swear to do all the training necessary to undo all the poor behavior my dog learned in its past life. Easy peasy!"

It's not easy peasy. It takes dedication, time, patience, skill, and more patience. If your dog is reactive to other dogs, you should stay off the trails until it can be relatively calm around other dogs. It means going to the park, day after day after day, and working through its issues.

It can take months and even years, and it's not something that you can work on once a week. It is a multiple times per day, lifetime commitment.

THINK SMALL DOGS CAN'T HIKE? THINK AGAIN!

I hike regularly with my friend Jessica and her two miniature dachshunds, Summit and Gretel. Admittedly, I was skeptical of their abilities at first, but after that initial hike, I never doubted a dog with short legs again. Together, we have gone on multiday backpacking trips and hikes totaling 10 miles. Summit and Gretel can keep up with my 45-pound dog with no problem. I must confess that I even feel a bit jealous over the amount of attention they receive on the trail. Everyone we pass comments on their bravado and ignores my dog!

CAN YOU HIKE WITH SMALL DOGS? ABSOLUTELY.

CONTRIBUTED BY JESSICA WILLIAMS

I'VE BEEN HIKING WITH SMALL DOGS, dachshunds specifically, for over sixteen years. I have learned a lot over the years, and use my experience to help others get outside and active with their own dogs through conversations with people who are surprised to see little dogs on top of a mountain and by sharing my tips and experience on my blog *You Did What With Your Wiener?*

When I started hiking with my dogs, I didn't realize that many people believed they didn't belong on the trails, based on small-dog stereotypes. I have made it my mission to prove that small dogs not only can hike, but also make wonderful trail companions. All dogs, regardless of size, need exercise, fresh air, and mental stimulation from exposure to new sights, smells, and environments.

Whether a dog will make a good hiking companion has more to do with individual personality, physical conditioning, and the fitness and energy required to do the job they were bred for, rather than size. For example, some dogs under 25 pounds, such as dachshunds, Jack Russell terriers, corgis, and Yorkies, were bred to hunt or herd and have a lot of energy and stamina. However, some larger dogs over 75 pounds were bred for guarding, or intense but short bursts of activity, and often can't hike for more than a few miles. Of course, not all small dogs like or are capable of keeping up with the big dogs, but in general that comes down to breed, training, and personality, not size.

10 Key Differences of Hiking with Small Dogs

1. It's easier to avoid tense confrontations with other dogs because you can pick them up if necessary, and it's easier to step aside on the trail.

2. There is less pet waste to pack out because their poop is smaller.

3. You don't have to carry as much dog food when backpacking because they eat less.

4. They may be small enough to fit inside your sleeping bag with you and help keep you warm at night.

5. They're easier to carry out in an emergency.

6. They're a great conversation piece on the trail because many people will be surprised to see them hiking and comment or ask questions.

7. Some obstacles may be too high for them, so they may need help up or down.

8. Small dogs are more affected by temperature changes.

9. They can't carry their own gear, or at least nothing of significant weight, inside a backpack.

10. They can be more susceptible to wildlife attacks because they aren't as intimidating and resemble small game.

Most Commonly Asked Questions

Q: "How can I start hiking with my small dog?"
A: Build up base fitness first by walking 30 to 60 minutes, four to five days a week, around your neighborhood or on easy dirt paths. Once your dog can do that, replace one of the weekly walks with a hike. Start with an easy trail of 2 to 3 miles and see how your dog does and if it likes it. You can progress to longer and more difficult trails from there.

Q: "How far can a small dog hike?"
A: In my experience, small dogs are capable of hiking the same length and duration a larger dog can. Both of my dogs have hiked 11 miles in a single day and 30 miles over a three-day period. I know of two dachshunds that have run a marathon and some small dogs that have hiked almost 20 miles in a day.

Q: "My small dog loves to hunt things in the woods. I'm scared he'll run off a cliff trying to chase something. Is my fear real?"
A: Yes, your fear is real. While your dog likely wouldn't jump off the cliff after wildlife, many cliff edges have loose rock and vegetation, so a dog could slip off the edge when trying to stop. The best way to prevent this from happening is to always keep your dog on a leash or to perfect your dog's recall so that they will come back to you every time, even if they are chasing something really exciting.

Q: "I have been using a retractable leash. Is that OK for hiking?
A: Personally, I don't recommend retractable leashes. They can invite behavioral issues like running up to other dogs or people without permission, can cause tripping hazards on the trail, and are thinner than a normal leash so they can snap easier.

10 COMMON MISCONCEPTIONS ABOUT DOGS

1. Dogs Need to Go to the Dog Park

There is a lot of debate about dog parks among the dog community. While many people love and visit them regularly, others avoid them completely. I am of the latter group. I find that dog parks are filled with dogs of varying energies and owners who are not fluent in dog language, a ripe scenario for dog fights.

Most trainers do not recommend them, because of the reasons mentioned above, and also because they deal with the aftermath of poor experiences. Further, you have no idea whether a dog inside the park has been vaccinated, and an unvaccinated dog can pass diseases like parvo, canine distemper, and kennel cough to other dogs.

What they are great for, however, is training for both humans and dogs. Humans can watch dogs interact to study how dogs communicate, and they are ideal spots to work on desensitization if you have a reactive dog, all while observing from outside the fence.

2. Dogs Need Other Dog Friends

Watching dogs play together can be an incredibly joyful experience, but dogs don't *need* other dog friends to live a fulfilled life. We've erroneously learned that "socialization" means to introduce your dog to as many people and dogs during a crucial period in its life as possible, but this just creates behavioral issues, as I explain in the section below.

It is a better idea to socialize your dog with dogs and people you know. You can facilitate a better experience with known dogs and people. Dogs don't need to meet all the people and dogs to be social. A few great experiences can be all you need.

Dogs can certainly have dog friends and can have close bonds with other dogs, but it is not a necessity.

3. Dogs Only Eat Grass When They're Sick

If this is true, then Sitka is constantly sick. He loves grass. He will go out of his way to find it on the trail. He will balance over a low bridge to get some of that green goodness. My friend calls grass snacking the "salad bar." Just try to prevent your dog from eating treated grass.

4. You Can't Teach an Old Dog New Tricks

I taught Sora numerous tricks in her final years, including some challenging ones like holding objects in her mouth. Tricks are a great way of keeping your dog's mind active and engaged, especially as its mileage decreases.

5. Dogs Get Plenty of Exercise in the Yard

The thought of a dog running around all day in a big grassy yard while you're away at work sure sounds like an ideal solution; however, dogs won't really just run around and entertain themselves in the yard all day while you're away. More than likely, your dog will just hang out or find ways to entertain itself by getting into trouble or through destructive methods.

The yard will quickly become boring to your dog. Dogs need to get outside of their home to experience new smells and stimuli to get the mental stimulation and socialization they need. If your dog is left unattended in the backyard, it can also practice negative behaviors like barking at passersby, which can lead to anxiety and leash reactivity.

Using the backyard as the main method of exercise also misses the opportunity to bond with your dog through play, structured walks, and training.

It's not uncommon for apartment dwellers to be rejected as potential pet parents because they don't have a yard for their dog. Dogs can absolutely live healthy and happy lives in apartments, often have stronger bonds with their humans, and receive more mental and physical stimulation than their canine pals with yards.

6. Your High-Energy Dog Needs to Run 10 Miles Per Day

Of course all dogs require daily exercise, but if you believe that you have to run your high-energy dog 10 miles a day to get it to chill out, then you're just creating an endurance athlete (which is fine, especially if you, too, are an endurance athlete).

The secret to a chill dog? Structure, routine, exercise, and mental stimulation. Implement the place training I discuss below. Create a routine for your dog, so they know when they will exercise daily. Give your dog puzzle toys or work on training in 10- to 15-minute spurts throughout the day.

7. Growling and Barking Indicate Aggression

On the contrary, growling and barking are ways that your dog communicates. Growling is a precursor to biting and should never be punished. A short, low growl means "please stop," while a longer, deeper growl means "knock it off!" Dogs will also growl out of discomfort, like when a stranger tries to hug or pet them in a way they don't like.

Barking can certainly be a nuisance, but sometimes a dog barks as a warning or to create space. If a dog is allowed to bark at, say, every passing human and dog, that's a problem, but when a dog barks at what it perceives as an unwanted visitor, that is a behavior some owners encourage. Since dogs don't know which strangers are actual threats, teaching the dog to stop on command will prevent unwarranted barking.

8. You Can't Train Certain Behavior Out of Dogs, It's Just Their Breed

While it is certainly true that some dogs come programmed with breed-specific behaviors (herder rounding up the kids at home?), it doesn't mean that you can't teach them when it is and isn't appropriate to employ these behaviors.

9. Dogs Love to Be Hugged and Kissed

I can't tell you how many times I have held my breath while my nervous dog pants atop a veterinary table as the vet cups its head in his or her hands and lays a giant smooch on its face. I'm also not sure how so many veterinarians still have their faces intact.

Some dogs will tolerate hugs and kisses only from the humans they trust, but the reality is that these displays of affection can come across as a threat. To show affection in dog language, sit together, play together, or groom your dog.

10. There Is Only One Way to Train a Dog

There is a lot of passion over training methods in the dog world. Many will argue for one way, claiming that other methods are abusive or suppressive. As a dog owner, you should do what is best for your dog, and if one method isn't working, then it's okay to do your research and explore alternatives. Dogs, like humans, are individuals and respond differently to different techniques. Learn what works best for the dog you have.

CHAPTER 2

SHAPING YOUR ADVENTURE DOG

BEFORE YOU SET FOOT ON THE TRAIL, plan to start working on your dog's obedience skills at home, indoors. By doing this, you'll avoid a lot of frustration (trust me), embarrassing interactions with other trail users (which are bound to happen at one point or another, no matter how well you train), and establish a strong bond between you and your dog.

OBEDIENCE SKILLS START AT HOME

The reason trainers start working with dogs indoors is because there are few distractions. Think of it like a buffet versus picking one item off a menu at a restaurant. Buffets can be overwhelming because there are so many options to choose from. You want them all.

When your dog goes outside the home, there are smells, dogs, wildlife, cars, people, urban noises, neighborhood sounds—dozens of stimuli that are competing for your dog's attention.

Starting indoors will help your dog master basic skills like sit, down, place, and focus with fluency so that when you do introduce distractions, it will be easier for your dog to cope.

PREPARING YOUR NEW DOG FOR HIKING

Whether you just added an adult dog or are waiting for the day that your puppy can *finally* join you on a proper trail excursion, there are heaps of ways to prepare your dog for the lifetime of adventures ahead.

If you have a puppy, the period before it is able to hike is the ideal time to work on obedience skills. The more you train, the more fluent your puppy will be when the time comes to hit the trails. A bonus is that training is *exhausting* for dogs.

I liken it to driving in the snow versus on a beautiful sunny day. In a snowstorm, you constantly have to think about keeping the car steady, looking out for ice patches, and maintaining a safe distance between you and the cars ahead. By the time you've parked the car, you're spent from all the mental work.

It's the same for dogs and training. I promise you, several 15- to 20-minute training sessions daily will tucker your pup right out.

The skills described below will get you off to a great start with your new adventure pal and give your dog a head start if you decide to work with a trainer. This will be hard work, but it's also a ton of fun and worth it for every time you hear someone tell you how well behaved your dog is. Those words are gold.

ESTABLISHING BOUNDARIES AND CREATING A ROUTINE

We love to treat our dogs like human children. We coddle them, spoil them, and give them privileges with abandon. This doting can, and often does, lead to behavioral issues. This is because dogs are not humans, they're dogs.

When humans don't treat their dogs like dogs, then the dogs become confused about who the leader in the relationship is and what the human expects of the dog.

This isn't to say that humans should not be affectionate with their dog; however, the affection should be earned and offered at the right time. For example, many dog owners will pet their dog and say "it's OK," in a soothing voice, while their dog is going ballistic at passing dogs. These owners are reinforcing this behavior in their dog, leading the dog to believe this is what is expected of it.

When you call your dog and it comes to you, that is an appropriate time to give affection and praise.

Each dog reacts differently to privileges. Some maintain wonderful behavior, while others turn into little monsters. If you have the latter on your hands, set some boundaries for at

least three weeks and see if you notice a difference. If all goes well and your dog has proven it's earned some liberties, you can gradually relax the rules.

What are some boundaries?

> The dog is not allowed on the furniture.

> You only praise and pet your dog as a reward.

> You calmly greet your dog when you come home with a simple "Hi!" as you would a human that you live with.

> The dog is not allowed to sleep in bed with you.

> Food is earned through obedience training.

> Nothing is for free—no ball toss without a command in exchange, no treat or food without earning it.

> No riling up your dog or using high-pitched voices to excite it.

> Give your dog crate time when you are home.

> Don't let your dog tell you when it's mealtime.

> The dog must respect thresholds (no bolting out the door or jumping out of the car without permission).

Setting these boundaries can be *incredibly* difficult for humans because we see them as our "fur babies." They're cute and we want them to feel at home.

Here's the thing: Dogs thrive on boundaries and routine.

Anxiety is amplified or created by a lack of structure and boundaries, and left to their own accord, dogs will set their own rules and resort to default behaviors like scavenging, peeing or pooping indoors, and chewing, especially when we leave them alone.

Structure shows dogs what is expected of them and alleviates the pressure to decide how to behave. Humans view freedom as humane and as a way to show love; however, freedom must be earned. Just like parents don't allow their children to run amok, dogs shouldn't have full reign of the house as they please either. Freedom is an earned responsibility.

Routines and boundaries help confident dogs learn that poor behavior doesn't get them what they want, and help anxious dogs learn to look to their human for guidance. Rules improve the relationship between a dog and its human, which is essential for an activity like hiking.

I had a trainer suggest these boundaries with a dog I once had, and the difference was incredible. Almost immediately, my dog began to respect me, she looked to me for guidance, and she was less reactive. Mind you, I had plenty of work to do with her elsewhere, but this step made a huge difference.

Eventually we were able to reintroduce some privileges like sleeping in the bed and hanging out on the couch. If your dog starts to take advantage of these liberties, then remove them.

SOCIALIZING YOUR DOG

Many dog owners have been taught that socializing their dog means taking it to the dog park and introducing it to as many dogs and people as possible in a short period of time.

Socialization refers to safe and positive experiential exposure. More exposure builds confidence, which is crucial for navigating the world as a dog. The key is to go slowly and set your dog up for success.

While puppies do have an impression period, all is not lost if your dog is not exposed to certain experiences during that time. I almost always adopt adolescent dogs, and while it may take more work to make up for lost time, it's not a total loss.

So, how do you properly socialize a dog?

How to Properly Introduce Dogs

Allowing your dog to go up to every single person and dog it sees will result in a dog that will protest when you do not allow it to meet every single person and dog it sees. This can foster leash reactivity and aggression.

Instead, arrange controlled introductions with friends and dogs you know. If your dog is reactive, find a friend with a calm dog to perform this exercise in the beginning. Two reactive dogs in the same space will just feed off each other, resulting in failure and frustration. Set your dog and yourself up for success on these introductions.

My preferred method, and one that I have had nearly 100 percent success (usually failure is almost always due to my mistake) with, is structured on-leash walks where the dogs do not interact with each other.

Start both dogs on leash and keep them at least 10 feet from each other, more if you see that one of the dogs requires more space.

A safe distance means that the dogs are not paying attention to each other. They are sniffing in their bit of space or sitting or lying down and waiting for the signal to go.

Signs that your dog requires more distance:

> It is staring intensely at the other dog.

> It is barking and lunging.

> It is not responsive to you.

Once everyone is ready, one team walks ahead, while the other follows behind, giving as much space as needed for the dogs to remain calm. This allows the dogs to share space in a safe manner while the movement keeps them occupied. Switch leaders every five or so minutes, and close the gap as the dogs become more comfortable with each other.

Eventually you can allow the following dog to sniff the leading dog's behind and then switch spots to allow the other dog the chance. Some dogs may be able to reach this step on the first day, while others may require a few sessions.

When you are bringing a new dog home or have a visiting dog, try to perform this exercise in your neighborhood before allowing the new dog inside your home. When you are inside the home, crate both dogs or tether them in place in the same room until both dogs are calm and comfortable.

Just Say No to On-Leash Greetings

For some reason, people assume that because they each have a dog, their dogs should meet. Society has created this expectation of dogs needing to socialize when, in fact, this is actually a very unnatural way for dogs to meet.

Dogs prefer to meet from the side, head down, with access to the rear. On-leash greetings do not generally allow dogs to interact in this manner and cause a lot more complications than most owners realize.

From the start, humans tend to miss key signals from their dog indicating whether or not it actually wants to meet this strange dog. Next, the owner gives in to undesirable behaviors like pulling, barking, whining, and lunging, which the dog has learned to use in order to approach other dogs.

Being tethered to a 6-foot leash prevents the dog from practicing avoidance behavior (flight) and does not allow them to flee if they have no interest in meeting the other dog. Instead, the owners are forcing the two dogs together in an awkward manner: face to face. An inability to flee the situation leaves the dog with only one choice: fight.

Leash tension can inhibit a dog's ability to effectively communicate to other dogs, resulting in mixed signals that can lead to aggressive behaviors. Further, dogs that desire space,

but cannot achieve it thanks to the leash, create the space by lunging and biting at the other dog.

In summary, on-leash greetings create stress for dogs by not allowing them to practice avoidance behaviors or to retreat in response to stress, leaving them no other option than to react.

Leashes also tend to become tangled as dogs dance around one another. This creates even less space for your dog to retreat if it prefers and puts everyone at risk of getting bitten should a dog wish to create space.

Avoid interactions with any new dog, leashed or not, especially when your dog is on leash. This means resisting social pressure and saying no to other owners when they ask. Dogs do not need to meet in order to satisfy socializing requirements. Rushing up to, greeting face to face, barking, and lunging are not normal dog greeting behaviors and should not be reinforced or encouraged. What is more valuable to your dog is learning to ignore other dogs as you walk by.

WHAT IS LEASH REACTIVITY?

HAVE YOU NOTICED THAT YOUR DOG seems to be completely fine meeting other dogs when they're off leash, but is out for blood when on leash?

This is super common among dogs—it is called leash reactivity.

If you watch two off-leash dogs interact, you'll notice a sort of dance they do. They circle around each other, sniffing various body parts, retreating when they feel the need. During this ritual, each dog is giving body language signals that keep the interaction in check.

On leash, this dance is controlled by the humans and a 6-foot leash, removing the fight or flight response. While the two dogs attempt the ritual, the leash becomes entangled or the dogs are unable to communicate effectively, leaving the dog in need of space no other choice but to create the space by growling and lunging at the other dog. Since the other dog is also stuck and tangled, a fight is inevitable.

It won't take long before dogs come to learn that snapping and growling will create the space they desperately seek during forced greetings. The aggression will be further reinforced by the owners, who now become nervous at the sight of other dogs, putting tension on the leash and sending stress signals to their dog.

Conversely, owners may (inadvertently) teach their dog to pull toward other dogs in a rude manner because it is allowed the freedom to approach other dogs at will. Now you've created a dog that becomes frustrated and throws tantrums when you take away this activity.

On-leash greetings are just one cause of leash reactivity. It can also occur as a result of:

› Previous attacks from other dogs

› Poor experience at the dog park

› Lack of structure and boundaries at home

› Strained relationship with its human

› Improper socialization

Leash reactivity is not only reserved in encounters with other dogs. Dogs can be leash reactive to a number of stimuli, including:

› Other humans

› Skateboards

› Bicycles

› Trucks

› Fireworks

› Other animals

As soon as you notice your dog starting to display reactive behaviors, talk to a trainer as soon as you can to nip it in the bud.

WHILE TRAINING FOR A MARATHON, I ran into a man walking fifteen dogs behind him. After I got over my initial shock, I noticed he was being followed by a small group of dog owners with their dogs as part of a group pack walk. When I learned that this dog trainer was providing this as a community service, I promptly signed up.

Sadly he left to move to the Wine Country, leaving a gap in our community. Not willing to let this stop me, I called on a friend and, together, we started our own pack walks.

Hannah explains what a pack walk is, how they benefit dogs, and how to start your own or join a local one where you live.

What Is a Pack Walk?

Pack walks are a great way to socialize your dog in a structured and safe manner. At its very core you're really just walking your dog with other dogs around.

The key difference in an organized pack or group walk is that the goal is to walk close enough for dogs to have positive interactions without actually coming into contact with one another. It's a fantastic way to socialize your dog and to capture and reward calm behavior.

You can look for pack walks on Meetup.com or on Facebook Events, or even your city's listings. If you don't have access to one, you can start your own.

Tips for Starting Your Own Pack Walk

FREQUENCY

Ideally you're walking once a week. A weekly pack walk has the greatest effect on a dog's ability to learn how to be calm around others.

LOCATION

Scout out locations in advance. Ideally the paths are wide enough that you can walk two to three dogs side by side and still have enough space for oncoming foot traffic. Varying up the locations each week gives the dogs the added challenge of being exposed to new environments.

LENGTH OF WALK

The speed at which the pack walks depends on how fast or slow the group moves together. Typically a walk lasting 1 hour is sufficient.

ORIENTATION

Anytime you have more than two dogs that have never met, you run the risk of a fight.

There is also a misconception among dog owners that our dogs need to "be friends" and "say hello." This couldn't be further from the truth. Allowing on-leash, nose-to-nose interactions with strange dogs is risky because you have no idea how your dog will react to the dog they just met.

We require all attendees to attend an orientation prior to joining our pack walk. This orientation is done in two parts. Each meeting notice has the rules of the walk, which we go over during the first 3 minutes prior to starting.

What Are the Rules?

We post all of our pack walks on Meetup.com, and below is a copy of our pack walk invitation.

We welcome *all* dogs, breeds, and temperaments.

However, please note that this means dogs of different skill levels. Some dogs may be at the canine good citizen level and others are at the "I need to learn social manners" level. The great thing is we are supportive of each other and respect where each of us is.

We'll start off with a 5-minute "short leash social" to establish calm energy and sit/stand as a group.

OUR GOAL IS TO

CONNECT with our dogs

CAPTURE CALM behavior

COEXIST as a group

› We discourage nose-to-nose interactions—refrain from introducing dogs until *after* the pack walk (we can provide a demo upon request).

› If your dog is vocal and likes to bark, please stand at the edge of the group so that he/she doesn't trigger other dogs. Also, please walk at the back of the pack.

› Only dogs that are up to date on rabies shots are allowed.

› *No retractable leashes* are permitted.

› For Dogs-In-Need-Of-Space (DINOS): If your dog is working on socialization, learning leash manners, or has anxiety or a medical concern, please *be safe* and do not interact with other dogs. Tie a yellow ribbon on your leash to signify your dog is a DINOS dog.

› You must supply your own poop bags and water.

› Maintain enough space between dogs so they are walking as close as possible without them having the impulse to smell each other. The goal is harmony and coexistence with space.

› We all walk at difference paces, but please *do not* pass the pack walk coordinator unless otherwise instructed.

› When a dog needs a potty or water break, we will all take a break together as a group; please do not pass others. Please yell out "BREAK" so that the group breaks together. Make sure you spread out during the break so that dogs have the space they need.

› Our goal is to walk as a pack—close enough for positive interactions, far enough as needed if your dog is reactive. We want our dogs to have a safe and structured social experience.

Additional Tips for a Successful Pack Walk

ARRIVE EARLY
Pack walk leaders should arrive at least 15 minutes prior to each pack walk so that they can greet early arrivals.

MAINTAIN A SMALL RATIO OF PACK LEADERS TO ATTENDEES
There should be at least two pack walk leaders to help monitor and guide the group. Limit your attendees to a level that you can handle, which could range from six to fifteen (maximum) per pack leader.

WATCH YOUR CITY EVENT CALENDARS
Be familiar with your city's events to prevent conflict with your organized pack walk. For example, one time we scheduled our pack walk during a 5K race, which made parking difficult for all involved.

KEEP ALERT FOR NON-PACK WALKING DOGS

Sometimes a dog that is walking with its owner and not part of the walk will want to say "hello." This oncoming dog might disrupt your group.

Alert the pack walk that there is an oncoming dog by simply saying, "Dog oncoming on the right," or whichever way they are coming from, and give the oncoming dog space.

Let the owner know to avoid your pack as well.

PACK LEADER POSITION

Ideally there are two of you handling the pack. One should be leading and the other should be toward the middle of the pack.

TAKE MULTIPLE BREAKS

Take two to three water breaks at predetermined locations that allow your group to spread out. Standing and practicing calm behavior for 2 to 3 minutes is also a great time to train your dog on how you want it to act. It's a good time to capture and reward this behavior with treats.

MIX UP WHO YOU'RE WALKING NEXT TO

Encourage pack walk attendees to mix up who they are walking next to after each break. This allows everyone to learn how to walk nicely next to another dog.

HAVE FUN

Not only are pack walks a great way to work with your dog, they're a great way to build community. Remember to stay relaxed and have fun during your walks.

TRAIN THE HUMANS IN YOUR LIFE

Dogs, and puppies especially, are stinking cute, and as much as I want to squeal and rub their bellies and baby talk to them, I refrain from doing so and I teach the people in my life to do the same.

When my dog meets new people, I ask them to ignore my dog. Don't look at it. Don't make high-pitched sounds. Don't say "hi." Act like there is no dog.

I begin all introductions with my dog in a sit, down, or in place, only allowing a greeting with permission on my release. And I *always* do greetings with people on leash while we're training, even (and sometimes especially) if they are someone my dog has already met. This helps curb jumping on people or reacting to unwanted interaction from the new friend. On leash, I can better engage my dog back to me to avoid undesired behaviors.

I ask my friend to continue to ignore my dog and let my dog inspect him or her. On my OK, I ask my friend to calmly pet my dog and continue to refrain from making high-pitched sounds. Save the squeals for training purposes. They make dogs overly excited and will encourage unwanted behaviors like jumping and biting.

After a few impressions, ask your friend to make squealing noises and engage your dog. Meanwhile, your job is to get your dog to bring its focus back to you, the handler, by asking for a "come" or "look" or another similar command.

EXPOSURE, EXPOSURE, EXPOSURE

A major part of the socialization process includes exposure to stimuli, objects, sight, sounds, and textures that dogs may find strange, fearful, or exciting. Dogs can be peculiar creatures, and some are more fearful than others, but here is a list of some common experiences dogs find scary:

> People in hats, sunglasses, big coats, talking loudly, etc.

> Surfaces like rocks, grates, bridges, and stairs

> Loud noises from fireworks, planes, trucks, motorcycles, etc.

> Strange objects like trekking poles, umbrellas, plastic objects (like tarps and mylar balloons), etc.

> Grooming procedures like toothbrushing, brushing, and nail clipping

> Wildlife (including urban wildlife like squirrels, bunnies, and house cats)

People who adopt often make the assumption that their dog was abused by someone it feared; for example: "My dog is afraid of men in baseball hats, so he must have been abused by a man who wore a baseball hat." Perhaps, but more than likely it is because your dog has just never seen a man in a baseball hat. Is he also afraid to see a woman in a baseball hat?

Early exposure will teach your dog that these sights and sounds are just part of everyday life. Practice patience with desensitization and stay at your dog's comfort level. Don't walk along the bike path next to the busy road on day one. Instead, follow the mail truck around the neighborhood from a safe distance.

ESSENTIAL COMMANDS FOR THE TRAIL

When you hit the trail with your pup, there are a handful of commands that your dog should be fluent with in order to avoid injury and damage to the environment, and to keep the peace among other users.

Every time I go for a hike or trail run, I use the opportunity to reinforce my dog's adventure skills by practicing the following commands throughout the adventure.

COME—If you want to hike with your dog off leash, then this command is not an option. Your dog must have impeccable recall, meaning they come on the first call, each and every time.

Some dog owners teach their dog an emergency recall, meaning they use that word sparingly, only when they need their dog to return urgently, say when they are about to approach a group on the trail or encounter wildlife. The key is picking a strange word you rarely use. I have a friend who chose the word "radish" as her emergency recall command.

PLACE—I had never heard of the "place" command until I had a hyperactive dog that would become overstimulated at the sight or sound of other dogs and people. Taking her to cafes was impossible, and she would shriek for a half hour straight if she met a new person.

This is my favorite skill to teach my dogs and is the first thing I teach them when I bring them home. Place means "stay in this spot and remain calm until I tell you otherwise." It's truly a magical command.

Karen Overall's Relaxation Protocol is a great guide for teaching place at home. Start out by practicing at home, in a nondistracting environment. I use an elevated cot so that my dog understands there is a clear boundary of where it should remain. You can also use a dog bed, and eventually other objects like towels, rocks, logs, and benches.

SACHI ABE

LEAVE IT—Your dog will encounter all sorts of new smells and tasty things on the trail. Some of these delights are poisonous and can cause serious harm or even death to your dog (see pages 73 and 127 for more information on trail hazards). Teaching "leave it" will allow you to have better control over the substances your dog inspects and tries to ingest. You can also simply use "nope!" which is my word of choice and encompasses a variety of "don't do that" commands.

WAIT—I use wait when I want my dog to stay where they are ahead of me on the trail. As an example, if I need to let my dog off leash in order to navigate tricky terrain, like a river crossing, I'll tell my dog to "go ahead," then ask for a "wait" while I cross.

SIT AND DOWN—I use these interchangeably on the trail and elsewhere. I personally don't mind if my dog is in a sit or down, it really just depends on the availability of space and the reactivity of my dog.

Down is generally preferred for more reactive dogs because it's a bit more relaxing than sit. In a sit, it's much easier for a dog to lunge at another dog than it is from a down position.

When someone is passing, with or without a dog, I always put my dog in one of these two positions, and if my dog is reactive, I face it away from the stimuli.

WHAT ABOUT STAY?—My trainer taught me to phase out the "stay" command. "Sit" means sit until I say otherwise, and the same goes for "down" or "place." I like this strategy because it reduces the number of words I need to bark to my dog (pun intended).

That said, stay is perfectly fine to incorporate into your dog's vocabulary, just be sure not to confuse it with "wait." Make sure you have a distinguishable difference between and use different hand signals for stay and wait.

THE ART OF THE STRUCTURED WALK

It's pretty impressive how strong dogs can be when they pull. I've been pulled by 10-pound dogs and by 100-pound dogs. Of course, the smaller dogs won't knock me down like a big dog, but walking with any dog that pulls is no picnic. It's unenjoyable and can cause injuries to the human.

Enter the structured dog walk.

A structured dog walk means that your dog is walking calmly by your side, focused on you and not distracted by other stimuli.

The rules are simple: no sniffing, no marking, no paying attention to other people, dogs, and sounds. To some, this may seem restrictive to a dog; however, dogs thrive on structure

and feel safe when their environment is under control. A structured walk will help build the bond between you and your dog, as you show your dog that you are the leader and will keep it safe.

In return, you agree to devote your entire focus on your dog. This means no phone, podcasts, or music, and no chatting with friends. These structured walks are just for you and your dog.

The goal is to keep moving forward. When your dog pulls or reacts to something, you pivot and head back in the opposite direction. Rethink your walk. Rather than your typical morning walk route, set your timer for 20 minutes and head outside with no agenda.

Two to three 20-minute structured walks daily will tire your dog like you wouldn't believe! It requires a lot of focus for your dog to keep its attention on you, which tires it out as much as an hourlong run, if not more so.

JEN SOTOLONGO

Don't think of these walks as a normal dog walk, rather think of them with the goal of getting your dog to walk with a loose leash. When I first started working with Sitka, we literally walked up and down the same stretch of a single block for 20 minutes.

Some dog owners may not be able to leave the house for those 20 minutes because their dog becomes too excited to go outside. In this case, you would walk around in your house and let your dog out only to go potty. A walk is a walk, even if it covers minimal ground.

The goal is to have a calm dog before you leave the house. Practice "down" with your dog with its equipment on in the house. When your dog is calm, it is then rewarded by going outside.

The calmness and confidence transfers wonderfully to the trail. Of course, your dog will be excited when you arrive at any new destination. There will be new smells from dogs and creatures gone before. Let your dog sniff around a bit to get it out of its system and enjoy the experience.

CHAPTER 3

WORKING WITH A PROFESSIONAL TRAINER

PREVIOUS: AMBER PITCHER; HANNAH ELLISON

I LOVE DOING RESEARCH. I will research something to death. I become obsessed with learning everything I can about the topic. I did this with dog training. I read the books, talked to friends and trainers, and watched the videos.

Then, I'd implement the techniques on my own dog and would have some success, but just couldn't achieve the same level of obedience as I could with a professional.

I felt like a failure the first time I decided to hire a trainer. I believed that I was incapable of training my own dog.

The moment I started working with a trainer, however, all those feelings changed to elation. I immediately saw how much better a trainer understands dogs. They know the precise timing for praise and corrections. They can predict behaviors better than I can. They know clever tools to use with your dog.

It was life changing.

Do remember, however, that a trainer can only work so much magic. It is up to you, the dog owner, to learn from your trainer and continue the work at home.

FINDING A QUALIFIED TRAINER

First, decide what your goals are for your dog. Do you want reliable off-leash recall? Do you need to work on behavioral issues like reactivity or overstimulation? Maybe you just want to start with the basics and go from there.

Once you have an idea of what you want to achieve and a style in mind, start your search. Here are some great places to look for a dog trainer:

> Ask friends in your region.

> Check Instagram and Facebook groups.

> Ask other dog trainers.

> Conduct a Google search and read through the reviews.

> Inquire at your local boutique pet store (avoid chain store pet training classes).

Once you've acquired a few recommendations, it's time to do your homework on potential trainers.

> Look through their social media pages and website. Do they show before and after? Are they educating their readers? Do they have a YouTube page or post videos of their work? Are they transparent about their training methods on their website?

> How much experience do they have?

> Schedule a consultation. Qualified trainers will ask you to fill out an intake form and then schedule a phone call or meeting to discuss your goals. Ask for references from previous clients.

> Ask them questions about their methods. Are they defensive with their replies? How do they interact with you, the human?

Dog training is not a regulated industry and anyone can claim to be a dog trainer. Make sure that you have a good match with your trainer before becoming invested in his or her

services. While there are certifications, I have found that I value the rapport I have with someone and proof of his or her skills from videos, referrals, and education more than I do letters behind the name.

LESSONS OR BOARD AND TRAIN?

Now that you've selected a trainer and identified the goals you want to accomplish with your dog, you'll need to decide if you want to do private lessons or send your dog to a board and train. Not all trainers offer board and train, but many do.

Board and train means that you will send your dog to the trainer's facilities for several weeks while the trainer works with your dog. This will achieve results more quickly; however, it is also more costly.

With private lessons, you will learn directly from your trainer, but will be required to implement the majority of the training at home using your limited knowledge.

Reactive, aggressive, and overly protective dogs will benefit most from a board and train, but it is entirely possible to do the work on your own under the guidance of a trainer. If you have the gumption, dedication, and time to work with your dog, then you can have success. It will take much longer to achieve results, yes, but you will also learn valuable skills as a handler.

MY PERSONAL DOG TRAINING STORY

Like many dog owners, I once firmly believed that positive reinforcement was the only and best way to train a dog. I believed that aversive tools like e-collars and prong collars were abusive and inhumane.

Then I had Laila.

Laila was a sweet and affectionate dog that loved all dogs and people. This caused her to go from zero to one hundred in seconds with overstimulation.

On the trail, she would disappear for 10 minutes if we let her off leash. On leash, she would pull so hard she lost her voice. She chased wildlife, jumped on people, and didn't listen.

And it wasn't for lack of training. I spent months working with her. We'd walk back and forth on our street to attempt loose-leash walking. We'd hit the park with a long lead and work on recall. I taught her place and fed her treat after treat after treat when we took her to a restaurant.

While my efforts made a small dent, she was just a wild dog that I didn't know how to communicate with. I would become instantly frustrated with her when I brought her along. I regretted bringing her on hikes or trail runs and would rather just leave her behind.

I had a dog I couldn't stand, and I felt like I had failed her.

One day I posted about my frustrations on Instagram. Dozens of friends and fellow dog owners commented that I should look into having her e-collar trained. I was shocked (yes, pun intended) to see so many suggest this method. These were friends I knew and trusted. They were people whom I knew loved their dogs more than anything.

So I looked into it.

I talked to friends. I consulted trainers. I watched YouTube videos from respected balanced trainers. I studied and I learned, quickly coming to the conclusion that I had been sorely misinformed by dog training marketing tactics.

JEN SOTOLONGO

While a breakup meant that I never had the chance to try an e-collar with Laila, we did start working with a trainer shortly before the end of the relationship to introduce a prong collar.

I remember arriving to our second lesson in tears. Laila was going ballistic as I neared the group of dogs. Still in positive reinforcement–only mode, I was stuck. If I moved forward, I'd be rewarding her behavior. If I stood still or turned around, we'd never make it to class.

My trainer spotted my distress, quietly came over and took her from me, and led her to class. He put a prong collar on her and showed me how to introduce leash pressure. She was almost instantly calm and manageable. I finally had a way to communicate with her, a way of letting her know what was and was not acceptable behavior. All my frustrations practically vanished with the introduction of one scary-looking tool.

I knew before I had even met Sitka that I would work with a balanced trainer to have my next dog e-collar trained. Because of the lifestyle I lead, the e-collar has been a life-changing tool. Sitka joins me on hikes and trail runs, running free off leash, and I can recall him on a dime any time I need. I don't panic if the leash comes unclipped or he takes off after a squirrel. I just push a button, which delivers a light stimulation that acts like a tap on the shoulder, and watch him sprint back to me, tongue hanging out. The tool gives me a way to have a conversation with my dog in a way that he understands, and in exchange we have built a strong bond based on effective communication.

I shared this story because I want to illustrate that there are different methods of training dogs. There is no one right way to train a dog, no matter what you read or hear from others. Dog training is complex, and every dog is different. I hope my story shows you that it is OK to go against everything you once believed if what you are doing is not working. You don't have to hate your dog, and you don't have to accept its behavior as it is in its current state. Do your research, ask questions, and come to your own conclusions.

CHAPTER 4
TRIP PLANNING

PREVIOUS: DEB BALCANOFF; KATHERINE TAYLOR

PLANNING HIKES THAT INCLUDE YOUR DOG is mostly similar to how you go about selecting them for yourself; however, there are some considerations to note before hitting the trail with your four-legged adventure buddy, such as regulations, weather, terrain, and athletic abilities.

FINDING DOG-FRIENDLY HIKES

It's easy to make the mistake of getting to a trailhead only to learn that it's not dog-friendly, especially if you're visiting a new area or are on vacation.

It's best to do your research before you head out to avoid having to turn around or try to find a hike on the fly. Fortunately, there are plenty of resources out there to help you find the perfect trail for you and your dog.

> › Official state park and federal government sites contain information about dogs, trails, and pass information.

> Hiking apps and websites are my go-to for finding dog-friendly hikes. You can sort by specific criteria, and some allow you to create lists to refer to for future hikes.

> Ask friends with dogs. I have learned about some of my most favorite hikes from friends. Those who are longtime residents in your region will know the trails best.

> Instagram and Facebook groups. Members provide great information about specifics that those hiking with dogs need to know, like whether there is shade, sketchy cliffside trails, or if the route is crowded during a certain time of year. Instagram dog accounts often keep favorite hikes a secret. If you live in the area and are interested in learning the location, make sure to engage with the account before simply asking for a location.

> Look for local blogs that write about dog-friendly hikes in the region. If you're in the Pacific Northwest, I know of a good one to check out (mine, longhaultrekkers.com).

> Ask a local tourism board. They know the ins and outs of their region, including lesser-known hikes. I used to work for one in Oregon and learned so much more than I ever would by just relying on apps.

> Get a paper map or use one online and simply search for trails and dirt roads. Sometimes the best discoveries aren't "real" trails. These are especially great for camping trips and finding isolation.

KNOW YOUR DOG'S LIMITS

Most importantly, when planning a hike for you and your dog, don't overestimate your dog's abilities and limitations (or your own, for that matter). Don't go out and pick a 10-mile hike if your dog has only hiked a maximum distance of 3 miles, six months ago. Like humans, dogs need endurance conditioning. They can indeed hike for long distances, but they need consistent training.

Some dogs will go on for hours, ignoring their body's signals alerting them of exhaustion. Other dogs lack confidence on rocks or steep terrain. Build their esteem by practicing on boulders in a nearby park. Learn your dog's behaviors and manage them appropriately.

Signs of exhaustion include:

> Excessive panting or labored breathing

> Bright red or purple, gray, or blue gums

> Haven't peed in a long time

> Rapid pulse rate

> Drooling

> Clumsiness

Some dogs can seemingly go on for hours swimming or playing fetch. They can't and shouldn't. Not only is this dangerous, but it also creates obsessive behaviors. If your dog is displaying any of the above signs, stop and take a break. If your dog is off leash, put it on leash and force it to slow down for a bit until it returns to normal. If you choose to let your dog back off, keep a sharp eye on its behavior and don't allow it to revert to what it was doing previously.

BUILDING ENDURANCE

Like humans, dogs need to build their endurance for hiking and other outdoors activities. Going too fast, too soon can result in injury and may deter your dog from enjoying your adventures because it associates them with pain or exhaustion.

Amber Pitcher and her rescued Siberian husky/lab/golden retriever mix, Ariel, live in upstate New York. Together, they have conquered both the Catskill 3500ers and the Adirondack 46ers, a mountain climbing club that requires summiting the thirty-five and forty-six peaks, respectively. When Amber adopted Ariel in 2007 as a junior in high school, she wasn't a hiker. It wasn't until she and Ariel accidentally summited two Catskill peaks, putting in 10 miles for the day, that they became hooked.

HIKING WITH SENIOR DOGS

As dogs age, the day eventually comes, always sooner than we hope, when they can no longer hike the same distances or jump the same heights. They amble much more slowly and rigidly and require more breaks. The fact that dogs simply do not live long lives is the most difficult part of having a dog.

It can be frustrating for sure to modify your more rugged outdoor pursuits; however, I encourage you to redefine the way you think about adventure. I can assure you that you will regret leaving your dog home for every outing more than you will having to adjust your plans for a few years.

Who knows, maybe it will even introduce you to a new activity that you love.

AS A HIGH-ENERGY AND PREY-DRIVEN DOG IN HER YOUTH, Ariel required plenty of exercise to keep her mind and body stimulated. We would spend our free time running through the fields, playing fetch, and exploring the trails that my father carved through our 30 acres of property.

Every day, Ariel and I would work on polishing her obedience skills, unknowingly setting the foundation for her adventure dog lifestyle. Daily training ensured that her recall was solid and her basic commands were flawless, while reinforcing our bond.

Eventually, we discovered local trails and nature preserves. After a couple of years of scouring all the local trails, we decided to branch out to find a new overlook with a view. Our overlook turned into summiting two Catskill High Peaks and a 10-mile day in the mountains. While I struggled and felt the fatigue from literally stumbling upon not only our first, but also our second mountain, Ariel was a complete natural in the woods.

After those first two mountains, I became addicted. Ariel's joy was evident and her grace in the mountains unmatched. I began researching the mountains in my state and found the Catskill 3500ers and the Adirondack 46ers hiking challenges.

The Catskills consist of thirty-five mountains over 3,500 feet, four of which require both a spring, summer, or fall climb, and another in the winter. The Adirondack 46ers include forty-six peaks over 4,000 feet.

In order to make those dreams come true, I knew we needed to prepare for the long days on the trail. The hikes would vary in length from 5 to 25 miles, and we could ascend anywhere from 2,000 feet to more than 10,000 feet in a single day.

Building Your Dog's Endurance for Long Hikes

To prepare for our hikes, I put Ariel on a training plan to build her up for the big days to come. Generally, Ariel was running one to three days a week, ascending high peaks once a week, and hiking smaller mountains or local trails two to three days a week.

With consistent training and adequate rest, Ariel has been able to accompany me on 20-plus-mile day hikes and is still happy and energetic at the end!

Obedience Training

Training may be one of the most paramount factors for hiking with your dog. Your dog should have strong obedience and recall skills before you decide to venture out into the mountains. Having your dog under control is key to having a safe and enjoyable experience for everyone.

Every day, Ariel and I would brush up on obedience training during a few short 5- to 15-minute training sessions throughout the day. I also enrolled her in professional training classes to ensure we both had all the tools we needed to succeed.

Start Out Easy

In addition to obedience training, physical training is also key to happy hiking. Your pup should not just be a weekend warrior. Just like humans, our dogs need to train for the mountains as well.

Start with smaller hikes to build up endurance. On weekends we would hike toward our club goals, generally working our way through our lists starting with easier peaks, saving the tougher ones for our peak fitness.

Put Together a Training Plan

I recommend writing out an exercise protocol for you and your pup so that you have something to stick to! Always remember to listen to your dog and its signals, because the last thing you want to do is push too far.

Incorporate Running

During the week, we would incorporate running days where we would run roughly 3 miles on a trail or a fast-paced mile down back roads in the morning before work. Running builds cardio strength and is just as good for your dog as it is for you.

Cross Training

Make sure your dog gets plenty of exercise during the week. Ariel and I included weeknight walks at local nature preserves, swimming days in warmer weather, and nightly games of fetch as part of our cross training.

Many of the peaks in the Adirondacks have obstacles along their trails such as steep ladders and exposed cliffs. Prior to those hikes, I had trained Ariel to climb ladders at home and had also taken agility classes with her. These were great ways to keep her confidence high, and when it came time to tackle those obstacles on the trail, she did so easily without any hesitation.

Food and Water

Dogs need fuel! For big days on the trail, I made sure to pack Ariel her own food and plenty of high-value dog treats. I recommend not feeding your dog a huge meal all at once, but rather providing small snacks throughout the duration of the hike.

Carrying extra water and offering it frequently is also essential to keep your dog well-hydrated and ready to trek through all terrain. Be sure to be aware of the available water sources on each hike, but do not rely on them solely for your pup's water. I always bring at least 2 additional liters of water just for Ariel, and often even more depending on the weather and the length of the hike.

Rest Days

While dogs do require some sort of daily physical activity, endurance athlete dogs should have at least one rest day per week, especially during peak training. Rest allows muscles to recover, reduces inflammation from strenuous efforts, and prevents burnout. Since our dogs can't tell us when and where they feel sore after a long hike, we need to build this into their training.

Great rest day activities include a short walk or an easy swim in the lake (not 30 minutes of fetch and sprints).

Hiking with Ariel, climbing all those mountains, and watching her navigate the most difficult terrain was seeing her in her natural element. It was like she was born to be a mountain dog. While our training and mindful prep was key to our success, Ariel also had such an affinity for the trails. She could problem-solve and route-find with ease, and her body seemed to be made for high-mileage days. Her muscles hardened, her paws became calloused, and her body was limber and graceful.

Ariel now has many mountains under her paws and has earned her way to fulfilling the requirements for a handful of mountain clubs throughout New York State and the Northeast. We have shared many active years and big days in the mountains together, something I will cherish through her senior years and beyond.

Continuing to keep your dog active is crucial for longevity, even as they slow down. I discuss several hiking alternatives later in this book, many of which are perfect for senior dogs, including:

> Car camping
> Watersports
> Swimming
> Short, flat walks
> Road trips
> Bicycle touring

AMBER PITCHER

RECOGNIZING SIGNS OF SLOWING DOWN

Aside from a slower pace, your older dog will start to display signs that it is no longer able to tackle the same journeys as it once was able to do. Keep an eye out for the following signs and take them as an indicator that you need to change the way you get outdoors:

> Hobbled walking or limping, signifying arthritis

> Heavy panting

> Clumsy agility (falling more often)

> Inability to jump onto higher obstacles

> Increased anxiety or fears

Each dog ages differently. My Aussie, Sora, as an example, joined me for multiple 20-mile runs in her final year, just before her last round of radiation therapy. She had plenty of energy and stamina still, even in her thirteenth year. Dogs that have joined their humans for endurance feats throughout their life will likely be able to continue longer than those that are more sedentary.

Starting your dog on a mobility supplement from a young age is a great way to keep those joints going strong well into their senior years.

ACCOMMODATING YOUR SENIOR DOG ON YOUR OUTDOOR ADVENTURES

When you do take your senior dog out for a hike, the following tips will help ensure an enjoyable and safe experience:

> **AVOID HIKING ON HOT OR COLD DAYS.** As with older humans, older dogs are more sensitive to extreme weather. Even moderately hot and cold days can be too much for your senior dog. If you are in doubt about hiking on a cool day, bring along a jacket for your dog and plan a short outing to see how it does.

> **ALLOW YOUR DOG TO STOP AND SNIFF.** We don't allow our dogs to use their sense of smell nearly enough. We become impatient and move them along. Give your senior dog the gift of experiencing more smells. Think of it like you scrolling through your social media. Smelling is a dog's version of this.

> **CHOOSE SHORTER, EASIER HIKES.** I often skip over short, easy hikes because they don't seem thrilling enough, but the senior dogs in my life have taught me that this just isn't true. Many waterfall hikes are short jaunts that lead to beautiful sights. Mountain lakes located just off the highway can have a jaw-dropping backdrop.

> **TAKE MORE REST DAYS.** Older bones and joints require more time to recover in between outings. If you head out for a short backpacking trip, consider staying for two nights to allow your dog a day of rest to recover before the return.

> **HIT THE BEACH.** Have you ever met a dog that doesn't love the beach? Nope, me neither! The beach is a wonderful place to play with senior dogs

and give them the opportunity to run at their leisure, taking breaks when they need.

UNDERSTANDING PUBLIC LANDS

Fortunately for dog owners, there are *plenty* of places to go hiking, many of which allow dogs off leash.

The US government manages 610 million acres of public lands, or 28 percent of the nation's landmass. Agencies from three different government levels manage these lands: federal, state, and local. Rules vary among the different designations, but there are some types of land that welcome dogs more than others.

Federal lands make up the majority of public lands (610 million acres) and are managed by four different agencies:

> Bureau of Land Management (BLM)

> US Forest Service (USFS)

> US Fish and Wildlife Service (USFWS)

> National Park Service (NPS)

For off-leash hiking and fewer crowds, BLM and USFS land is your best bet. Concentrated largely in the western United States, USFS and BLM lands make up 441 million acres, or nearly 70 percent of public lands.

Each management system sets different goals for designating the land as one type over another. BLM and USFS objectives include recreation, sustainable resource harvesting, and conservation.

BLM land tends to be located in less-populated areas with more primitive recreational opportunities, allowing dogs off leash in the undeveloped areas.

In contrast, USFWS and NPS lands are more restrictive to dogs, since their main objective is protection for future generations. While there are a handful of national parks that are more dog-friendly than others, the general rule of thumb is that dogs must stick to the most developed areas, usually paved paths.

While restrictions vary from state to state, and even among different parks in the same state, state parks are another wonderful dog-friendly option for hiking. Most will likely require leashes at all times.

PERMITS

Many lands require permits for day use or overnight permissions. Again, this varies by state, but check before heading out to the trail so you're not at risk for getting a much more expensive ticket.

Most popular trailheads will include a pay station where you can purchase a day pass, but if you live in or plan to stay in the same region for a period of time, it makes sense to look into annual passes. They can usually be purchased at a number of locations including outdoor recreation stores, grocery stores, and ranger stations.

WEATHER CONCERNS

Enjoy year-round hiking with your pup, but take the necessary precautions when it comes to weather. Fall is a favorite season for many hiking enthusiasts. Parents and kids are back to work and school now that summer vacation has ended, and the trails are a little quieter.

Springtime welcomes new blooms, and with those come the April showers. Hiking during the spring often means lots of mud, both from rain and melting snow from the winter season.

The summer and winter months require a little more planning, thanks to extreme heat or cold. Go prepared and you'll be able to enjoy hikes throughout the year.

SUMMER HIKING

Hot summer weather can result in serious health conditions for your dog, like heatstroke, dehydration, or even death. For some dogs, temperatures above 75°F can be too much, so it's important to take note of the temperature and monitor how your dog performs in the heat.

Hike in the Morning

Temperatures are significantly cooler in the morning, especially just before sunrise, since the sun has been down for several hours. Personally, the early morning is my favorite time to get out for a hike because most people would rather stay in bed, leaving the trails nearly empty.

Pick Hikes with Water Access and Shade

Depending on your location, try to find hikes with access to water and plenty of shade during the summer months. The shade is often 10 to 15 degrees cooler than direct sunlight, which can make a huge difference for your dog's comfort.

Another way to beat the heat is to go up in altitude. In sunny conditions, the temperatures can decrease 5.4°F for every 1,000 feet in elevation. However, keep in mind that going up may also mean less tree coverage and more intense sun, resulting in sunburn on sensitive areas like a dog's nose, the pink around its eyes, or any other areas where it may not have fur.

Like humans, dogs can get altitude sickness, so take precautions and acclimate if you plan to go higher than 9,000 feet above sea level.

Great options for summer hikes include:

> Wooded trails

> Coastal trails

> High-altitude hikes

UNDERSTANDING THE SIGNS OF HEATSTROKE IN DOGS

Dogs exposed to excessive heat can suffer from heatstroke. Left untreated for too long, heatstroke can lead to seizures, coma, cardiac arrest, and death. If you notice any of the signs below, remove your dog from the heat immediately and cool it down gradually using a fan, wet towels, or air conditioning. Cooling a dog down too fast can actually cause the internal organs to heat faster and shut down.

› Rapid heart rate

› Excessive panting

› Heavy drooling and/or thick saliva

› Red or pale gums and tongue

› Dizziness

› Extreme fatigue

› Vomiting

› River hikes

› Lake destinations

Hikes to avoid:

› Fully exposed trails

› Trails composed mostly of rock, like in Arizona or the northeast United States

› Hikes with no water access

› Trails with a lot of pavement

Bring a Cooling Vest

Several outdoor dog gear companies make cooling vests for dogs. These are light gray–colored jackets that help keep your dog cool. Just submerge the vest fully in water, wring it out, and secure it on your dog.

The material deflects the sun and draws heat from your dog's body as water evaporates in a middle layer of the vest. On hot days, the vest will dry out fairly quickly, so plan to hike near water to continue soaking the vest.

Another tip is to keep a wet washcloth or small towel with an ice pack in a cooler in the car. This way you can cool your pup down when you arrive at the car after a warm hike.

WINTER HIKING

The colder months are a great time of year to get outside and take advantage of less-populated trails. Not only that, but dogs love the snow, and nothing will abolish those winter blues like seeing your dog run zoomies in the snow. Another bonus is the extra calories you'll burn as you trudge through waist-deep snow.

As with summer, you'll have to make some planning adjustments to ensure a safe and enjoyable experience for both you and your dog.

Jackets and Sweaters

Dogs with double coats like huskies, Samoyeds, and other northern breeds are well equipped to handle cold temperatures for longer periods of time than, say, dogs with shorter coats, like chihuahuas and terriers.

What this means is that you may want to consider getting a winter jacket for your dog if you plan to hike throughout the year. In the past, dog jackets were more about fashion statements than practicality, but as more dogs accompany their humans on their outdoor adventures, dog jackets make more sense.

Some dogs, no matter the coat type, tend to accumulate snowballs that attach to their fur like burrs. Because they freeze to the fur, removal requires melting. You can avoid snowball-velcro syndrome a couple of different ways:

> Outfit your dog in a snowsuit or sweater that fully covers its chest, legs,
> and belly.

> Take some coconut oil and rub it on the part of your dog's fur where snowballs tend to accumulate and comb it through. The coconut oil acts like a repellent for the snow.

Paws

Dog's paws can form painful ice balls that build up in between their toes. If you notice your dog limping during a hike in the snow, check for ice balls and try to remove them gently.

If your dog has a tendency to accumulate ice balls, consider getting a pair of winter trekking booties, or use a preventive wax-based paw balm like Musher's Secret to deter them from accumulating in the first place.

Water

Waterways may be frozen during the winter months, plus winter hiking requires more exertion and often the air is dry, meaning dehydration is a concern.

Bring along extra water for your dog, and don't forget a portable water bowl.

Eye Protection

Have you ever gone skiing and removed your goggles after spending some time on the slopes? It's blindingly bright. Like humans, dogs may require eye protection from UV rays. Dog goggles not only look super cool, but they also serve an important purpose.

Certain breeds of dogs or those with light-colored eyes are more prone to eye diseases like pannus and sunburn. If you have any of the breeds listed below and hike regularly, consider getting your dog a pair of Rex Specs dog goggles:

> Border collie

> Lab

> Weimaraner

> Australian shepherd

> Husky

> Corgi

> Dachshund

> German shepherd

> Greyhound

KNOW SYMPTOMS OF HYPOTHERMIA

A dog's normal body temperature ranges between 101 and 102.5°F what humans would consider a fever. Just a difference of a few degrees can mean a dangerous hypothermic situation for your dog.

Prolonged exposure to cold is an obvious cause of hypothermia. Parents of young and senior dogs need to be extra vigilant, as they are at a higher risk since they lose body heat more rapidly through their skin.

Symptoms include:

> › Shivering and trembling
>
> › Pale gums
>
> › Lethargy
>
> › Frostbite, especially on the paws
>
> › Fur and skin are cold to the touch
>
> › Decreased heart rate
>
> › Body temperature below 97°F

Bluebird skies and high elevation can cause sunburn, particularly in dogs that have exposed skin around their eyes.

Dog Bed and Towel

If you plan to stop for a little bit to eat lunch or sip on a warm beverage, pack a lightweight travel dog bed to give your pup an insulated place to lie down or sit while you take a break. A dog's body temperature cools quickly in cold weather, which can cause hypothermia.

You can also bring a warm beverage, like bone broth, for your dog, and carry it along in an insulated thermos.

Packing a small towel allows you to wipe off excess snow or water from streams as you hike, which will help prevent your dog from becoming excessively cold.

WINTER TRAIL HAZARDS

No matter how well you may know a trail during the remainder of the year, everything changes completely with snow present. Bridges are slick, trees are weighed down with

snow and more susceptible to falling, and icy conditions could pose a danger for both you and your dog.

Further, winter conditions create hidden hazards like tree wells and snow bridges over waterways. Your unknowing dog could easily fall in and become stuck or injured or drenched in icy water, putting it at risk for hypothermia.

Always check avalanche conditions the morning before you head out to the trail. Even if you checked the night before, there may have been overnight snow accumulation where you're headed.

Local avalanche centers should have the most updated information. Otherwise, call the regional ranger station for the most up-to-date information. When in doubt, stick with lower-elevation hikes and always tell someone where you're going.

UNDERSTANDING SIGNS OF FROSTBITE

When the temperature drops below freezing, dogs can experience frostbite. Exposure to extreme cold will result in reduced blood flow to parts of the body. The most commonly affected regions are the paws, ears, and tail.

Signs of frostbite include:

› Pale gray or blue discoloration of the affected area

› Affected area feels cold to the touch

› Pain with touch

› Swelling of the affected area

› Blisters

› Blackened or dead skin

As with heatstroke, it's important not to warm your dog too quickly, as that can result in shock. Instead, apply heat using the following method:

› Remove your dog from the cold.

› Dry your dog using a towel.

› Wrap your dog in a dry towel, dog bed, coat, or whatever you have until you can get back to the car.

› Back at the car, turn the heat on and warm the towel or blanket on the heater as fast as you can, then wrap your dog in it once it's warm.

› If you brought a hot beverage, transfer it to a non-insulated vessel, wrap it in a towel, and apply it to your dog's stomach.

› Offer your dog a warm fluid to drink, like broth or water.

Monitor your dog constantly. If you have a thermometer, recheck its temperature every 10 minutes. Schedule an appointment with your vet to check for any long-term damage or if your dog has not recovered after 30 to 45 minutes.

OPPOSITE: LAURIN SMITH; STACI KATES

BUILDING ENDURANCE

Hiking in the snow is more akin to walking in sand dunes or wading upstream—it requires a lot more effort than a walk on pavement or on an easy dry trail. This means that both you and your dog will expend more energy during a snowy hike.

If your dog is not used to harder endurance outings, take a few weeks to gradually build its strength and prepare for winter conditions.

PLAN ACCORDINGLY

Since the days are much shorter during the winter months, planning accordingly means avoiding getting stuck out on the trail when night falls and the temperatures really drop. Remember that darkness descends in the woods earlier than in urban settings, so plan to turn around well before sunset.

Always pack a headlamp and lighted collar for your dog just in case there's a mishap and you find yourself walking back in the dark.

CHAPTER 5
TRAIL ETIQUETTE

THE TRAILS BELONG TO ALL USERS. It's especially important for those hiking with dogs to remember this. All too often a dog comes barreling down the trail from behind a hidden bend headed straight toward another user and his or her dog.

Meanwhile, there is no owner in sight.

Or, the owner shouts something along the lines of, "Don't worry! He's friendly!" Sometimes, the owner just calls the dog's name over and over and over and over, while the dog completely ignores its owner. Even worse, the owner just stands there and does nothing.

A dog running wild ruins hikes for other users, and is rude and dangerous. Often, when a managed dog reacts by lunging or even biting, that dog is unfairly blamed for the reaction, when they are simply creating space.

Many new dog owners see other folks let their dogs off leash and follow suit, not knowing any differently. Set a good example and manage your dog when you hit the trails.

MANAGING YOUR DOG ON HIKES
CONTRIBUTED BY DAWN MELLON

AS MORE PEOPLE HIT THE TRAILS with their canine companions, it's becoming more important than ever to exercise proper etiquette when encountering other hikers with or without canine companions. So what do you do when you see a fellow hiker approaching?

First of all, no matter what your feelings are about how friendly your dog is and whether or not you believe in leashing your dog while hiking, you should 100 percent of the time have your dog under control and not permit it to approach another person or animal without consent.

No one should have to interact with your dog unless they choose to. It's beautiful when dog owners work together to peacefully pass each other and avoid interactions when it is clear the interaction is not desired.

Step one is to train your dog to respond to your "come" command so it is under control while off leash.

When you see a person and/or dog approaching, call your dog to you and leash it. If your dog is not comfortable with dogs or people coming into its space, then it's your job to find a way to create space. Look around to see if there is a wider area with a durable surface where you safely step off the trail with your dog.

As you step to the side of the trail, use treats to keep your dog's focus from locking onto the passersby and continue to reward it as they pass by. Rocks or large trees make great natural barriers. For dogs that love to play, you can often also use toys as a distraction from the passersby.

If you do not have a lot of space to work with, move your dog to your side on the outside of the trail. Assuming people follow natural movement on the right-hand side of the trail, move your dog to your right side so your body is between it and the oncoming hikers.

Providing a buffer can offer your dog more security and prevents the person or dog reaching for your dog as they pass. If you do not have a lot of space, and provided the footing of the trail is adequate, usually passing quickly is going to work better than trying to get your dog to sit and stay while someone passes by very closely. Use treats to help guide your dog past.

The key to using treats successfully is to start giving them before your dog reaches threshold rather than trying to use them after your dog is already amped up. When you go to pass, make sure you have the leash held securely and close so

if your dog lunges you are ready to stop it, but try not to keep the leash tight the entire time as you approach, as this can cause more tension.

If you are on an incline, traditional hiking etiquette would be to yield to the person traveling uphill. But with passing dogs, it is far easier to be pulled off balance by a dog going down an incline. Therefore, the uphill hikers should continue to move forward while the ones descending should pull over to the side to avoid falling.

If you are hiking with a nice friendly dog and see that another person with a dog sees you, calls the dog, puts it on leash, and steps off the trail, this is your cue to please leash your dog and move by. That behavior tells you the person does not want to meet or say hi and likely has a dog that might get upset or too excited. You can really help the situation if you quickly move on by, keeping your dog under control. Please also keep in mind that even with friendly dogs, people can be injured by getting run over, by dogs playing and running into people's legs, and so on. If space allows, try to keep your dog a leash length's distance away from passersby.

It's a good idea, if the trail permits off-leash hiking, to keep your dog leashed and focused on you for a bit after the passerby goes by, as many dogs will want to go back to see who just passed and will race away when you take the leash off. It's also good practice not to let your dog go around blind corners without you, in case someone is right there.

> If someone asks you to leash your dog, then do it without opposition.

> If someone asks you to recall your dog, then do it without opposition. If your dog does not come, then physically walk (or better yet, jog) up to your dog to leash it or take it to the side of the trail.

> Do not allow your dog to approach other users without permission.

> Do not allow your dog to run ahead, out of sight, and then shout, "My dog is friendly!" when you see other people or dogs approach. It doesn't matter if your dog is the friendliest creature on earth. There is a time and place to share that love, and unsolicited greetings on the trail are not it.

OFF-LEASH HIKING

Off-leash hiking is a privilege, not a right. It takes a lot of practice, patience, and dedication to shape a reliable recall. What exactly does "reliable" mean?

It means that your dog doesn't tear off into the woods or run down the trail completely out of sight once it is free. It means that your dog doesn't go up to other dogs and people without permission. It means that your dog comes all the way to you when called the first time, without stopping to pee, sniff, or say hi to other dogs or people, and then it stays at your side until released.

Dogs that cannot do this successfully nearly 100 percent of the time should not be hiking off leash. Uncontrolled off-leash dogs can:

> Frighten other users

> Cause leash-reactivity

> Start fights with other dogs

> Undo hours upon hours of training with one wrong move

> Cause injury to others

> Make hiking an unpleasant experience for other people

> Destroy sensitive habitat

Not only is this inconsiderate to other users, it is dangerous. Your dog may indeed love all people and other dogs, but that doesn't mean those dogs and people love your dog.

Owners who choose to hike with their dogs off leash must manage them 100 percent of the time. What this means is that they need to keep an eye and ear out for voices ahead and animals in the woods. They need to learn to read their dogs' body language in order to predict their next move.

It means putting your dog first, even if you are hiking with friends. You may not be able to participate fully in a conversation, or may have to stop speaking mid-sentence or interrupt your friend in order to recall your dog. If you can't focus solely on your dog or are not willing to do so, then your dog should remain on leash.

Be honest about your dog's abilities and keep it on a leash if it doesn't have stellar recall.

Yes, it's great fun to have your dog off leash and watch it run free and sniff everything in sight, but if your dog is not yet under voice control, then it has not earned the right to be off leash.

Just because your dog is on a leash doesn't mean that it can't have a good time. Even on leash, dogs can enjoy a sensory experience by sniffing. Whenever I feel annoyed when my dog stops to have a good sniff, I remember that this behavior is like scrolling on social media for dogs and allow a few minutes every now and then on the trail.

"WATCH OUT, SHE'LL TURN ON YOU ONE DAY."

The words of a passing hiker infiltrate my ears. Though I keep my cool and pass without response, I feel a wave of anger wash over me. Comments like this are just some of the many I have experienced since I adopted a pit bull–type dog in 2013.

Leilani (Lani) is my first dog as an adult. Unlike many of my friends, I had no breed expectations. My husband, Brian, and I simply wanted to adopt a dog that fit into our lifestyle. When the time came, Brian and I chose the dog we bonded with at the shelter and paid no attention to how they labeled her. That said, I've always been attracted to bully breeds. I love their big blocky heads, short fur, athletic build, and how their bodies never seem to stop wiggling. It's only fitting that we came home with one. Bringing a pit bull–type dog into an apartment with breed restrictions posed an entirely different set of problems, but that's for another time.

Admittedly, I had a glorified idea that she would innately be the perfect hiking companion. Naively, I thought she would walk calmly next to me. This was not the case. I severely underestimated the amount of work and training it took to have an appropriate trail dog.

Our first time on the trail, an elderly gentleman stopped to say hello. I watched Lani's body fold into a beautifully executed play bow, and, thankfully, the man was very understanding when she exuberantly mistook his trekking pole for a stick and pranced off with it.

Not everyone is as forgiving; I learned this the hard way. A few years ago I thought she was ready for off-leash hiking. It was a foolish mistake, as her recall was nowhere near perfect. After failing to return to me, she intercepted someone's picnic and scored a sandwich. The poor, unsuspecting person was upset, and understandably so. The thing is, they weren't upset that she was off leash, but that she was a "pit bull" off leash.

Another time, we were the recipient of an off-leash dog that did not end well. The other owner was quick to place blame, pointing out that pit bull–type dogs tend to be dog aggressive due to their history of dog fighting. He recommended I leave my dog at home where she belonged. This really hurt. Had I really failed to socialize my dog? Or did decades of breeding predispose her to this behavior? Would we be able to hike together like I had always dreamed?

Every unwelcome experience led to the profound realization that I carried a heavier responsibility than the average pet owner. Somehow, a pit bull barreling toward a picnic poses a much greater threat than say . . . a bichon frise.

Knowing I had much to learn, I delved into the world of canine language. I absorbed every word of every book and article I could get my hands on. I made a commitment to training, one that would last her lifetime.

Together, we practiced walking on a loose leash and passing other dogs without engaging. I began to see the ways she was communicating with me and her environment. I stopped allowing her to greet other dogs on leash. When you think of a reactive dog you think of barking, lunging, snapping, and snarling. Lani doesn't do these things, which makes it difficult for other owners to discern her level of comfort.

I became very in tune with the more subtle cues that she generously doled out. With humans, she is excited and wiggly and welcomes the scratches and pets. Other dogs are a different story. She gives excellent calming behaviors such as sniffing the ground, averting her gaze, licking her lips, and yawning.

When those appeasement cues fail to reduce her discomfort, she begins to posture and her eyes grow wide. Though her tail wags, it's raised high and stiff. Every single one of those behaviors demonstrates (or should) that she would not like to be approached. I do my best to create positive, safe spaces for her on the trail. We often hike on weekdays at or near sunrise, when the trails are less busy, and I always carry treats. Just because a dog tolerates certain scenarios does not mean they are comfortable doing so.

The truth is, I didn't really understand my dog until I stopped trying to fit her into a mold and accepted her as an individual. To answer my questions above: It's absolutely crucial to socialize dogs and give them a positive environment. It's also important to consider genetic components that can play a crucial role in temperament and behaviors. But neither genetics nor environment are exclusive in shaping a dog—the two are fluid. This is the single most important lesson I learned as a dog owner.

So, what is it like hiking with a pit bull–type dog? It's like hiking with a best friend.

ADVOCATING FOR YOUR DOG

Your job, as your dog's guardian, is to speak up on its behalf, learn to communicate with it, and protect it from harm. The skills explained below will enable you to advocate for your dog.

LEARN TO SPEAK DOG

Dogs communicate extremely well. Humans just aren't as fluent in dog as we expect our dogs to be of our own language. It is only fair that if we ask our dogs to learn a bit of our language, that we learn some of theirs in return.

It is the duty of handlers to learn their dogs' signs of distress, stimulation, fear, and anxiety to keep them safe. By understanding our dogs' needs in a given situation, we can then give our dogs what they need to reduce their stress.

COMMUNICATE CLEARLY WITH OTHER PEOPLE AND DOG OWNERS

Speaking up for your dog can be incredibly difficult, especially if you're introverted, shy, or just don't want to portray your dog as an angry beast. However, if you value all the work you've put into your training, then practice speaking up. More importantly, if you have a reactive dog that could hurt someone, you could be saving its life and preventing injury to others.

A few key phrases that work well include:

"My dog is not friendly with other dogs."

"Would you mind leashing your dog?"

"Can I pet your dog?"

"No, I'm sorry,

. . . we're training."

. . . he is afraid of children."

. . . he is resting right now."

"Can our dogs meet?"

"No, I'm sorry, we don't do on-leash greetings."

UNDERSTAND THE RISKS OF HIKING OFF LEASH

There will be some people who will tell you that your dog doesn't belong on the trail. Maybe it's because your dog is reactive. Maybe it's because of the breed. I will tell you this: If you manage your dog when you hike, keep it on leash if it has not earned off-leash privileges, and you are a courteous trail user, then your dog has every right to be on that trail.

In fact, hiking on shared trails is a great way to help reactive or anxious dogs gain confidence around other dogs, if done correctly. Ironically, the problem often isn't your reactive dog, it's the unmanaged "friendly" dogs.

Unfortunately, many (many) dog owners abuse off-leash rights, making hiking stressful for other users, particularly those with dogs.

If and when you choose to hike with your dog off leash, know that you run the risk of encountering other off-leash dogs whose owners don't follow the same training protocols as you do.

The entitled dog owners on the trails have decided that the rules do not apply to them. They can be aggressive and even dangerous, and so can their dogs. I have been screamed at and insulted by other dog owners, all because I asked them to leash their dog and they refused. Most of the time, their dog has no recall at all.

It's not a matter of if this scenario will happen, it's when.

That said, I still choose to hike with my dog off leash, when I feel it is safe to do so. It also means that I wake up at the crack of dawn on weekdays and drive farther distances in order to minimize my interaction with other users.

Use your best judgment and be prepared to protect your dog as best you can. There will be uncomfortable interactions and times when you have to make a decision that may seem mean or will anger the other dog owner. You are well within your rights as the owner to protect your dog from other off-leash dogs by any means necessary.

How to Manage Uncontrolled Off-leash Dogs

The most stressful part of hiking with a dog is encountering unmanaged off-leash dogs. There will be times when the owner is not doing his or her job and you'll have to step in to do it for that owner, especially if one or both dogs are reactive.

When you encounter an off-leash dog approaching and your requests to the owners have gone ignored (by either them or their dog), do everything in your power to keep the strange dog away from yours. This could mean:

› Standing tall, putting your hand up in a "stop" position, and saying "NO!" in a firm voice

› Using a stick, trekking pole, or umbrella to keep the dog away from yours

› Tossing a handful of treats toward the strange dog and away from your own dog

› Using Pet Corrector or citronella spray

› Tossing your keys toward (not at) the offending dog

› Squirting or splashing the dog in the face with water from your bottle

In cases when you encounter an aggressive dog with the intent to harm, you may have to resort to more extreme methods:

› Kicking the other dog

› Hitting it over the snout with a stick or other object (while ensuring to keep your hands clear)

› Spraying it with pepper or bear spray

There will be people who completely ignore you or owners who have no control over their dogs, and uninvited encounters will happen. Try your best to avoid these situations using the tactics described earlier in this chapter and in chapter 6, Hiking with a Reactive Dog.

Others will mutter to their children that your dog is mean. Some will think that you are incredibly rude. It's annoying but completely OK, because it really doesn't matter what they think. It matters that you speak up for your dog and continue on your way.

NONVERBAL CUES TO AVOID INTERACTION WITH OTHER DOGS

Before I had a dog of my own, I had no idea of the quiet communication that occurred between dog owners. Upon seeing another dog and its human coming down the sidewalk in an opposing direction, I'd notice them quietly escorting their dog across the street in order to avoid interaction.

This wasn't personal, it was just a way to avoid interaction between dogs.

I noticed the same on the trails and began to learn from other dog owners. Sometimes, handlers need to put their entire focus on their dog and are not able to communicate verbally with others. The following cues are signs that they do not want other dogs or humans to approach:

> If the trail is wide enough, cross to the other side and keep walking, stationing yourself between your dog and the strange dog.

> Step off the trail, put your dog in a sit or a down, and use your body to block the approaching dog from greeting your dog.

> Use the "place" command on a nearby log, rock, or other elevated object to create space between the other dog.

> Completely ignore the other person and dog. Unless you need to communicate that you do not want them to approach, do not otherwise engage.

> Explicitly declare that you or your dog do not wish to be approached. Respect this request if you hear it.

PAY ATTENTION TO THE ENVIRONMENT

Whether my dog is on or off leash, I keep a sharp eye and ear out for other dogs and people, sounds, bends in the trail, obstructed views, children, and so on. I am always scanning the environment so that I can adjust our plan accordingly.

If I can't see around a bend or over a crest, I recall my dog. If I hear sounds in the distance, we pull off to the side and I put my dog in down to allow the users to pass. I am always ready to react at a moment's notice and create the space my dog needs in order to maintain the trust it has in me.

It can be exhausting at times. It sometimes means that I cannot give my full attention to my human companions on busy trails or those with obscured views.

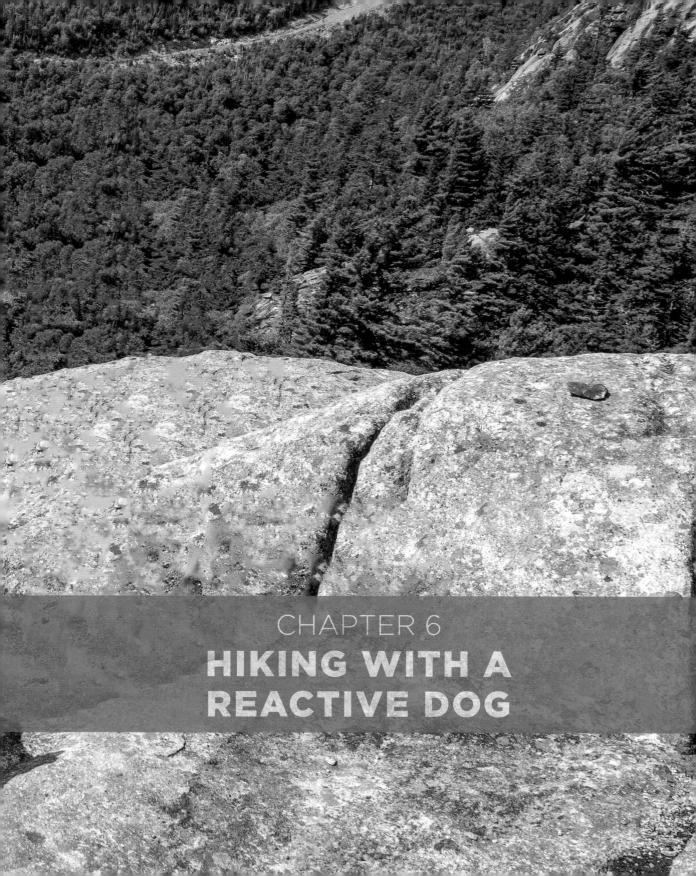

CHAPTER 6

HIKING WITH A
REACTIVE DOG

HIKING WITH REACTIVE DOGS CAN BE incredibly unpleasant and challenging. Not only are you having to navigate off-leash dogs barreling down trails where leashes are required, you also have to manage your dog around distractions and triggers, like other people, wildlife, and other dogs.

I have a very soft spot for reactive dogs. Every dog I have had has been a reactive dog. Reactivity can either show in the form of lunging, growling, or biting to create space, or it can also show as overstimulation with excessive barking, shrieking, or "tantrum throwing."

I have learned everything that I know about dogs from my reactive dogs. They teach us to be really in tune with their needs, pay attention to the signals they give off, and anticipate reactions before they happen.

I could not write this book as it is today without my reactive dogs.

If you have a reactive dog, an alternative is to plan to hike very early in the morning or evening or during the week, if your schedule permits, to avoid other dogs.

PREVIOUS: DEB BALCANOFF; JURA CRAVEN; OPPOSITE: KATELYN WARD

HELPFUL TIPS FOR THOSE HIKING WITH REACTIVE DOGS
CONTRIBUTED BY RORY RILEY TOPPING

IF YOU'VE EVER BEEN TO THE CITY OF BOSTON, you know that its culture is basically the antithesis of southern charm. People are in a hurry, they're direct, and if they're displeased, they'll tell you. Exhibiting similar characteristics is how my blue Doberman, Boston, earned her name.

In the dog world, however, having these traits is often labeled as reactivity. Boston certainly fits the criteria for a reactive dog—she is sensitive to the presence of other dogs and stimuli, meaning she will bark, lunge, or otherwise "react" to things she perceives as invading her personal space.

As you can imagine, hiking with a reactive dog can be challenging. Most of us, whether accompanied by our dogs or not, hike to relax and enjoy the great outdoors, and feeling threatened by a strange dog does just the opposite—it can be quite stressful.

Nonetheless, one of the best ways to help a dog with reactivity is continued exposure to stimuli and desensitization. Here are some tips to make hiking with your reactive dog a less stressful experience for you and those around you:

› **CHOOSE THE ROAD LESS TRAVELED.** Yes, certain hiking trails are popular for a reason, but sometimes large crowds can complicate a dog's reactivity rather than present a training opportunity. By choosing a trail where you are less likely to encounter large crowds of people and other dogs, you can be more aware of your surroundings and prepare for how to handle those passing by with other dogs.

› **HIKE AT OFF HOURS.** Trails tend to be most crowded on weekends, holidays, and late afternoons when the average person is off work. If possible, hike early in the morning or midday when you are less likely to see large crowds. As mentioned above, this provides the best opportunity to be fully aware of your surroundings and plan accordingly.

› **HAVE A PLAN.** Having a friend with a dog who is willing to help you practice before you hit the trails can be very helpful. For

us, our plan typically involves stepping to the side and creating space, if possible (this is not always possible on narrow trails, particularly if sensitive vegetation is nearby). Space is our friend, and enough space can help us avoid a reactive episode altogether. However, when this is not possible, we work on distracting Boston by training a "look at me" command (dog should focus on you, not the approaching dog) and rewarding with copious amounts of treats (i.e., eye contact and engagement is rewarded, reactive behavior is not). Conditioning a routine like this makes it easier to apply when encountering strange dogs on a hiking trail.

> **SEEK OUT TRAILS THAT REQUIRE DOGS TO BE LEASHED.**
> Of course, not everyone obeys leash laws at all times, but most
> people want to obey the law and enjoy the outdoors responsibly.
> When other dogs are also leashed, this can help prevent unwanted
> encounters with other dogs from escalating by ensuring that
> everyone keeps a safe distance.

> **DON'T BE AFRAID TO USE YOUR VOICE.** In dog culture, we
> often assume that all dogs want to be friends. In the same way that
> I do not want to interact with every person I see on a trail, chances
> are, your dog doesn't either. So if people ask if their dog can say
> hello, don't be afraid to say no thank you. I typically say something
> like "my dog isn't good with other dogs" or "we're training and
> don't want to be approached." Most people are receptive to this.
> Similarly, if you see an off-leash dog approaching, don't be afraid
> to yell out to the dog's owners and ask them politely to leash their
> dog or reiterate that you do not want to be approached because
> your dog is not friendly or you are practicing training.

> **MUZZLE-TRAIN YOUR DOG.** Although there is still a stigma
> associated with muzzles, they are a great tool to promote safety
> for your dog and others. Sometimes dog reactions can escalate
> into dog fights, and if you have any doubt about your ability to
> prevent such an escalation, use a muzzle. Muzzles have many
> other benefits—they can be helpful in medical emergencies and
> can prevent your dog from eating things off the ground as well.
> Boston uses a standard Baskerville plastic muzzle on some hikes
> if we think there is any chance of a potential safety issue. Plus, the
> more people who advocate for muzzle training, the more we will
> accomplish to erase the stigma!

In an ideal world, you will be able to practice these steps enough times that you
can work through your dog's reactivity and no longer have issues while hiking.
However, working with a reactive dog is a slow process that takes patience. For
example, Boston is 5 years old, and although her reactivity has lessened due to the
steps mentioned above, we have not yet totally eliminated her reactive behaviors.
Even though we still have work to do, we still lace up our hiking boots and make
sure we get out there!

MUZZLES

If you have not had a dog in your life that has required a muzzle, your first thought when you see a muzzled dog walking down the street or coming down the trail is probably along the lines of, "Oh, that is a very aggressive dog and I need to stay far away."

   Muzzles certainly carry a number of assumptions and look scary, but in reality they are important tools used by many dog owners to keep their dogs, as well as other dogs and people, safe.

DON'T FEAR THE MUZZLE
CONTRIBUTED BY JOANNA LEE

KANE, MY 6-YEAR-OLD MIXED-BREED DOG, is my hiking partner; he will go all day, climbing challenging terrain, running up steep elevation gain, and scrambling through and over obstacles, all while giving me 100 percent enthusiasm and effort.

He absolutely loves every second we spend hiking in the woods or the mountains. However, Kane isn't always an easy hiking partner. He is very uncomfortable around unfamiliar dogs and people when they invade his space. Since we cannot control the actions of other people and their dogs, this is one of the reasons we embarked on a muzzle-training journey.

Why Muzzle Your Dog on the Trail?

Muzzles are used by many people for a wide variety of reasons, but the primary goal is usually safety, whether that applies to your dog, other dogs, or humans. If you encounter a dog on the trail wearing a muzzle, it does not mean this dog is a bad dog or an aggressive dog, but it may mean that dog needs a bit of extra space today. A muzzled dog is a safe dog!

Some dogs, like Kane, are nervous and uncomfortable with new dogs or new people. It is inevitable that we will encounter other people and dogs on hikes, some of whom allow their off-leash dogs to approach and invade our personal space. We also encounter people who want to pet every dog they see.

Both of these situations make Kane very uncomfortable and sometimes, despite our extensive training and my warnings to the approaching hiker, I cannot prevent these situations from occurring. In such circumstances, he may lash out or make his discomfort known loud and clear by showing his teeth, barking, and lunging at approaching off-leash dogs.

While the muzzle doesn't silence his discomfort, it does ensure that no dog or human is harmed.

Other Benefits of Muzzling Your Dog on Hikes

In addition to safety purposes, muzzles also come with a few other benefits:

› **THEY CAN DETER OTHER USERS FROM APPROACHING.** The muzzle can serve as a visual cue that a dog may not be comfortable interacting with people or dogs and needs extra space. This helps keep us, other hikers, and other dogs calm, safe, and happy.

› **WE CAN SAFELY SPEND TIME IN THE OUTDOORS WITH FRIENDS AND THEIR DOGS.** We enjoy sharing our love of nature with friends. Since moving to Colorado we have met many new friends who also enjoy hiking with their dogs, which served as another incentive to muzzle-train Kane. Muzzles ensure safety for everyone when introducing and hiking with multiple dogs, some of whom may have behavioral issues.

› **MUZZLES PREVENT DOGS FROM INGESTING TOXIC SUBSTANCES.** Another important reason for using a muzzle while hiking is because some dogs will unwittingly eat anything and everything in their path. Some of these things may be toxic or poisonous, and some may require surgical removal. While most muzzles allow dogs to be fed from your hand, they prevent them from picking up potentially harmful objects off the ground.

Muzzle-Training Tips

While it might initially seem like a daunting training goal, it is absolutely possible to have your dog be comfortable in a muzzle. Introduced in a positive manner, your dog won't mind wearing a muzzle in many situations, including hiking. Here are a few pointers that worked well for us:

› **FIND A MUZZLE THAT FITS CORRECTLY.** The right size will sit snugly, but not too tight, on a dog's nose to allow panting and water and food intake.

› **MAKE IT FUN!** If other types of training with your dog can be fun, why shouldn't muzzle training be fun, too? Go slowly and make it a positive experience to ensure that your dog sees the muzzle as an accessory that means adventure time.

› **START IN A LOW-DISTRACTION ENVIRONMENT,** such as your house, and progress slowly to wearing it outside the house. In the beginning, reward your dog for any interaction with the muzzle, like a paw or nose touch. Next, insert a treat inside the tip of the muzzle or hold one just outside, so they have to stick their nose inside. Eventually you can progress to snapping the muzzle in place, so they get used to the sound of the clip and the feeling of the straps.

› **BUILD UP DURATION OVER TIME.** Saving meals for training is a great way to progress. Feed your dog by hand while wearing the muzzle. Start to ask for behaviors, like sit, shake, or other tricks. Next, take your dog outdoors and play with it while wearing the muzzle. Your dog may only allow a few seconds of wear in the beginning. That is OK. Keep at it.

› **IF YOUR DOG SEEMS UNCOMFORTABLE IN THE MUZZLE,** just take a step back in the process and work at its speed.

CHAPTER 7

PRACTICING LEAVE NO TRACE PRINCIPLES WITH DOGS

FREQUENT VISITS FROM MILLIONS OF PEOPLE can wreak havoc on trails, destroying habitats, damaging historic artifacts, causing wildfires, and more. Users are responsible for their own actions, including those of their dog. The Leave No Trace Center for Outdoor Ethics guidelines help minimize visitors' impact on the outdoors. While geared toward humans, dog owners should adapt and apply Leave No Trace principles for their dogs in order to reduce impact.

PLAN AHEAD AND PREPARE

Read trip reports before you head out so that you know exactly what to expect when you arrive. Will there be snow? Is it going to be hot later in the day? Is there water along the route?

Knowing this information will allow you to prepare as best you can and hopefully avoid any emergency situations happening out in the wilderness.

Always make sure to tell a friend or family member where you are going, when you plan to leave, and your expected return time frame.

UNDERSTAND AND OBEY THE RULES

There will always be rule-breakers, and, unfortunately, dog owners, not their dogs, are often the culprits. Since dogs are not aware of where they can and cannot be off leash, it is up to individual dog owners to follow the rules and set examples for other users. If a dog causes trouble, it's not the dog's fault.

Encountering off-leash dogs on hikes that require a leash is almost a guarantee on most trails these days.

Seeing one dog off leash gives other visitors the impression that their dog can be off leash too, resulting in more dogs off leash on restricted trails. What this means is that other users can't enjoy the trails, and other dog owners hike with stress wondering when they'll run into an uncontrolled off-leash dog.

Leash rules are made to protect natural areas, keep people and other dogs safe, and limit damage to trails. Most hiking sites indicate whether a trail permits dogs off leash. Check before you go to manage expectations.

LIMIT HIKING IN LARGE GROUPS

Group hikes can be a fun way to meet new people and help socialize a new or reactive dog. Keep in mind, however, that large groups can dominate the trails. If your group exceeds more than six people and dogs, spread out into smaller groups so that other hikers are not inundated with loud conversations and packs of dogs.

TRAVEL AND CAMP ON DURABLE SURFACES

As idyllic as it sounds to pitch a tent or picnic in a meadow filled with wildflowers, doing so causes damage to the vegetation, and blazing a trampled path invites other users to follow

your footsteps. The Leave No Trace Center for Outdoor Ethics recommends camping only on rock, sand, ice and snow, dry grasses, and gravel.

If you are planning to camp, picnic, or enjoy a view, stay on existing paths and established campsites. Set up camp at least 200 feet from lakes and streams.

If your dog tends to wander off the trail, it's best to leash it in particularly sensitive areas, including wet meadows, living soil found in desert regions, wildflower fields, and anywhere there is low vegetation.

DISPOSE OF WASTE PROPERLY

Dogs have an uncanny ability to hold their bowels in the trailhead parking lot and then decide to release them just far enough away from the trailhead trash bin. Now you're faced with a few options:

> › Carry the bag of poop with you the entire hike.
> › Walk back to the trailhead and toss the bag.
> › Leave the bag on the side of the trail and pick it up on your way back.

Option three is a fairly common practice, but not the ideal choice. Poop bags left on the side of the trail are unsightly to other users, and they are often left behind because the owner has forgotten about the bag after several hours of hiking.

For those averse to the idea of stuffing a bag of poop into a side pocket, there are a few options:

> › Bring a water bottle reserved just for poop bags. Don't forget to label it as such!
> › Transfer the bag to a Turdlebag or another stink-free bag.
> › Stash it in your dog's backpack, if it is wearing one.

LEAVE WHAT YOU FIND

Dogs love sticks and digging. While this is great fun for them at home, try to limit their digging and stick destroying on the trail or on banks along rivers and lakefronts.

WHY DO WE NEED TO PICK UP DOG POOP IN NATURE?

Wondering why you have to pick up the poop in the first place? Wild animals don't have a human collecting their waste, so why can't dog poop decompose like the rest of the animals' poop?

Wild animals consume food that comes from their environment, so when they poop, they are simply returning the same resources back to the ecosystem.

Pet dogs, however, eat dog food. Kibble contains nutrients like nitrogen and phosphorus, which can cause algae blooms and invasive species, both of which negatively affect native species. Additionally, dog poop contains bacteria, which can spread disease, pollute soil, and contaminate our drinking water.

Dogs produce 10.6 million tons of waste each year. In Boulder, Colorado, alone, dogs leave behind 30 tons of waste annually. Now imagine if all dog owners refused to pick up that poop or left it in little bags on the sides of the trail.

There are no dog poop fairies (though sometimes I play the role). Picking up and carrying poop is a reality of dog ownership.

STAY ON THE TRAIL

If you hike with your dog off leash, ensure that it remains on the designated trail. Allowing your dog to wander off the path causes damage to the flora and fauna. Your goal should be to leave the trail in the same condition, if not better, than when you arrived. Dogs can break sticks, trample on plants, and scare wildlife.

TAKE CONSCIOUS PHOTOGRAPHS

Since Instagram came along, people are flocking to photo-worthy destinations, causing damage to sensitive wildlife ecosystems and even causing injury to themselves or their dogs. During the 2019 poppy super bloom in California, tens of thousands of people went in search of the flowers.

While not a crime to visit, many trampled on the plants in order to take a photograph, not realizing that doing so prevents future growth.

Learn photography methods of capturing the image while remaining on the trail.

RESPECT WILDLIFE

It's important to remember that when you hike in the woods, you are visiting the home of the native animals that live there. Dogs with prey drives or that become excited by new sounds can startle wildlife, frightening the animals and ruining the viewing experience for other users.

CHAPTER 8
HEALTH AND SAFETY

WHETHER YOU ARE HEADED OUT FOR a short day hike on a trail you've hiked a million times or venturing on a multiday adventure, preparing and packing for emergencies and understanding the trail hazards are essential to the health and safety of your dog.

This section discusses the essential gear and skills you need to have and know before you head out on the trail with your pup.

THE 10 ESSENTIALS FOR HIKING WITH DOGS

Though rare, trail emergencies do happen, and bringing along the 10 Essentials for both yourself and your dog will keep you safer than if you were to enter the wilderness without them. In the West, in particular, wildfires can trap people in the mountains, storms can hit at a moment's notice, or injuries can prevent movement until help arrives.

The list of 10 Essentials overlaps some for dogs and humans, and you want to ensure that you have both.

Humans will want to bring the following:

1. Navigation tools (map, compass, GPS device, etc.)
2. Headlamp + extra batteries
3. Sun protection (sunscreen or a hat)
4. First-aid kit
5. Knife or multi-tool
6. Fire (matches, fire starter kit, stove, etc.)
7. Emergency shelter (simple bivy sack or light tarp)
8. Extra food
9. Extra water
10. Extra clothes

The list for your dog varies some and is more specific to their needs, of course, including:

1. Pet first-aid kit (which can be combined with the human one as long as you make sure to include pet-specific items)
2. Booties (for any injuries that might prevent your dog from walking)
3. Extra food
4. Light-up collar or light attachment
5. ID tag
6. Water + water bowl (in a pinch, you can use a poop bag)
7. Dog bed or jacket
8. Sun protection (cooling vest, dog goggles, and pet-safe sunblock for dogs with visible skin)
9. Extra poop bags (or a small trowel to bury the poop)
10. Harness with a supportive handle for lighter dogs, and emergency harness for heavier dogs

PET FIRST AID

Carry a first-aid kit with you that includes supplies to treat both you and your dog. Familiarize yourself with the contents and learn how to use them. Ask your veterinarian if they offer first-aid courses or check for a class in your region. I purchased the e-book version of the *Field Guide to Dog First Aid* by Randy Acker to refer to on the trail.

Items to include in a dog first-aid kit:

> Blunt-end scissors
>
> 3% hydrogen peroxide (to induce vomiting in case of poison ingestion)
>
> Saline eye cleaning solution
>
> Disposable gloves
>
> Gauze
>
> Oral syringe
>
> Antiseptic gel
>
> Benadryl (and knowledge of your dog's dosage)
>
> Alcohol wipes
>
> Medical tape
>
> Tick removal device
>
> VetWrap
>
> Styptic pencil
>
> Space blanket

In addition to carrying the items listed above, here are a few additional items to consider bringing along:

> MUZZLE: In the event that your dog is in pain or shock from an injury or bite, there is a high likelihood that it will become agitated and bite you or anyone attempting to help. A muzzle will prevent bites. Part of this safety measure is in the preparation. Don't expect a dog to be happy being muzzled for the very first time in a state of stress. Familiarize yourself and your dog with the muzzle before you hit the trail. If a dog is already in a stressed state, trying to put a muzzle on when it doesn't want something on its face could be detrimental for both the human and the dog.

JOANNA LEE

> **BOOTIES:** Bring along an inexpensive pair of booties to protect torn or raw paw pads. Dogs build endurance and calluses on their paws, but they may develop cuts and tears in the beginning stages. If your dog cannot walk on a severely torn pad, then it's going to be a long and slow carry back to the car (trust me, I've been there).

> **RESCUE HARNESS:** For those with larger dogs, consider carrying a rescue harness, like the Fido Pro. If your dog breaks its leg or is unable to walk due to injury, a rescue harness will enable you to carry your dog back down the mountain to safety and medical care. The harness works as a sling that allows you to carry your dog either on your back or in front, sort of like the baby-wearing products available to parents.

> **KNOW THE NUMBER FOR THE NEAREST VETERINARIAN:** If you are not hiking in an area where you would normally take your dog to the vet, then make sure to know and save the number for the nearest veterinarian in your phone. If you are hiking on a weekend or hiking after hours, then look up the number and location of the nearest emergency veterinarian.

UNDERSTANDING THE TRAIL HAZARDS THAT COULD HARM YOUR DOG

You may be surprised to learn that some of your favorite hikes might contain plants, insects, and other parasites that are toxic to dogs. The hazards vary from region to region, so it's important to familiarize yourself with the threats in the area you plan to hike.

Do your research on potential toxins if you plan to visit a new hiking area in a different ecosystem. This knowledge could save your dog's life!

WATER FROM STREAMS AND LAKES

Like humans, dogs can contract diseases from bacteria in water, such as giardia, cryptosporidium, and leptospirosis, to name a few. While dogs' stomachs are stronger than those of humans, it doesn't make them immune.

Plan to pack a separate water bottle for your dog on shorter hikes. On longer treks, bring a water filtration device to provide fresh water.

KATELYN WARD

SALMON POISONING

Salmon and other upstream swimmers can become infected with a parasite called *Nanophyetus salmincola*. This parasite is relatively harmless, however, when *that* parasite becomes infected with another one called *Neorickettsia helminthoeca*, then it becomes potentially lethal for dogs.

Salmon poisoning is most common west of the Cascade Mountains in Washington, Oregon, California, and southern British Columbia. Dogs are the only animals susceptible to the infection.

The problem occurs when dogs eat raw salmon at places like riverbanks and oceans. When a dog ingests a salmon carrying the infection, it causes systemic complications. Symptoms include:

> Vomiting and diarrhea

> Lack of appetite

> Swollen lymph nodes

> Dehydration

> Fever

> Weakness

Since the symptoms can be rather general, telling your vet that salmon poisoning is a possibility could help save your dog's life.

RATTLESNAKES

Found across the United States, though most common in the American Southwest, rattlesnakes can be a deadly threat for hiking dogs. Surprise encounters or prey-driven dogs cause snake bites that can be lethal without immediate medical attention.

Rattlesnake bites are painful, life threatening, and can cause permanent damage even if the dog does survive. While there is a vaccine that helps decrease the severity of the reaction against some types of rattlesnake bites, it is not a preventive measure. It really only buys your dog a few hours. The protection lasts six months, so regular boosters must be administered to produce the antibodies.

With the right support and treatment, the majority of dogs do survive rattlesnake bites. However, owners must get their dog to a veterinary clinic as soon as possible. Treatment is not cheap. Antivenom costs anywhere from $450 to $750 per vial. Smaller dogs may require several doses.

If you are hiking in an area known to have rattlesnakes, take precautions and manage your dog with a close eye.

> Stay on the trail.

> Keep your pet on a leash or close to your side.

> Do not let your dog sniff in holes or rocky areas, dig under rocks, or run through grass.

> Keep an ear out for a rattling sound.

> If you spot a snake that also sees you, keep your distance and give it time to escape. It doesn't want to interact with you unless it feels threatened.

> Dead snakes may still contain venom, so keep your curious pup away.

JURA CRAVEN

If you live in an area where rattlesnakes are common, consider attending a rattlesnake avoidance class. The classes introduce your dog to live, muzzled rattlesnakes in a contained setting while using an e-collar to associate your dog with the sights, smells, and sounds of the rattlesnake.

The training uses low-level stimulation to teach your dog to avoid potentially harmful situations with rattlesnakes. Many pet owners decline to use e-collars in most situations. When it comes to rattlesnake safety, this training can truly be lifesaving. Weigh the options carefully, especially if you and your dog hike often in rattlesnake country.

TICKS

Ticks are small blood-sucking insects found across the globe, and dogs are magnets for these little critters. Many tick species transmit diseases like Lyme disease and Rocky Mountain spotted fever to both dogs and people.

Ticks must be attached for 36 to 48 hours in order to transmit Lyme disease. Signs include swelling in dogs' joints, fever, or lameness and take two to five months to present. Lyme disease can lead to kidney disease, which can be fatal for dogs. Most prevalent on the East Coast, Lyme disease is now found in every state in the continental United States.

Rocky Mountain spotted fever is one of the more commonly seen tick-borne diseases in dogs. Symptoms include fever, lack of appetite, swollen lymph nodes, and joint pain.

Ticks tend to hang out in tall grass, fallen leaves, and shrubs and bushes. Dogs are more susceptible to attracting ticks when off leash, since they probably go off trail and sniff around in tick habitats.

Check your dog for ticks after a hike by massaging their body, paying special attention to areas like the belly, the ears, face, between the toes, and the tail. If you spot a tick, use a tick key to remove it, taking care to include the head. Symptoms may not present for seven to twenty-one days, so keep an eye out for changes in behavior or reduced appetite.

The best way to prevent ticks on your dog is to use flea and tick medications. There are both natural as well as chemical-based methods for flea and tick prevention. Depending on where you live, choose your preferred system and apply diligently.

Natural remedies include sprays, ingestible powders, and specific foods that repel bugs.

There is also a canine vaccine available for Lyme disease. Talk to your vet to learn which products work best in your region.

COMMON PLANT SPECIES TOXIC TO DOGS

Since plant species vary across different environments and regions, familiarize yourself with those that are potentially toxic to your dog. Different plants cause varying degrees of toxicity, including kidney failure, nausea, vomiting, liver failure, coma, and even death.

To help with plant identification on the trail, consider downloading an app to help you determine whether a species may be harmful to your pup.

The list below includes some common plant species that can affect dogs:

> Foxglove

> Lily of the valley (all species of lilies are poisonous to dogs)

> Bleeding heart

> Rhododendrons

> Bluebells

> Crocuses

> Daffodils

> Elderberry

> Ivy

> Mountain laurel

> Mushrooms

> Foxtails

PET INSURANCE

It's becoming more and more common among dog owners to purchase pet insurance for their dogs. Adventure dogs especially have higher risks of injuries and ingestion of poisonous plants like those mentioned above, simply because they are more exposed and engaging in more extreme activities.

There are a number of pet health insurance companies out there today, most of which offer several different plans based on what works best for your budget and lifestyle. Your quote is determined by the age and health of your dog.

It can be a bit of a process to choose the right pet insurance. Ask friends what they use and get recommendations from them.

Veterinary care is not cheap, especially if you have to take your dog to the emergency vet. Insurance will ensure that you don't have to suddenly find the cash or go into debt to save your dog's life and could allow you to keep your dog on the trails with you for the long term.

FUELING YOUR TRAIL DOG

Endurance athletes require a lot of fuel and water, and dogs are no different. More active dogs will need to replace calories lost from exercise, as would a human who trains for an ultramarathon.

Highly active dogs may require up to 25 percent more calories than the typical amount (2 percent of their body weight) recommended for the average dog. Talk to your vet about how many calories you should be feeding your dog during high-activity seasons. If your dog appears a little thin, then add a bit more; too pudgy, then reduce.

CHAPTER 9

CAMPING WITH DOGS

DOGS MAKE WONDERFUL CAMPING COMPANIONS and seem to enjoy sleeping outdoors just as much as humans. Of course, some dogs may require a few trips to learn to tolerate the different sleeping arrangements and sounds, so practicing before heading out is a good idea for those with anxious or more alert dogs.

TIPS FOR CAMPING WITH A DOG

Sleeping outdoors introduces new stimulants for your dog. There will be sounds and smells they've never experienced, there may be wildlife they've never encountered, and there could be other humans around, depending on where you spend the night.

PREVIOUS: JEN SOTOLONGO; ALYSSA SALAVA

PRACTICE AT HOME FIRST

Before heading out for a night under the stars with your pup, practice at home several times until your dog feels comfortable sleeping in the tent. It may seem strange to pitch a tent in your living room or the backyard, but it's actually a lot of fun!

Start with a few nights indoors before setting up the tent in your backyard. This way, there will be fewer new stimulants than if you were to head straight outdoors first.

PACKING DOG FOOD

Packing dog food is as simple as measuring out the food into a plastic bag or small, sealable container and feeding your dog as usual. If I am car camping, I am less precise about measuring, as long as I ensure that I have at least an additional day's worth in case of emergency.

For backpacking, I like to measure out the exact amount I need plus add a day or two in case of emergency or if I decide to stay longer. I keep the food in zip-top bags and write the amount inside each bag for reference.

For those who feed raw, look for freeze-dried or dehydrated mixes, and be sure to pack enough water or camp near a water source so you can rehydrate the food at mealtime.

When you go to bed, treat dog food like your own food and put it away in a critter-proof container or in your car. I have woken up to a raccoon feasting on my dog's food just outside my tent!

STAYING HYDRATED

Always make sure to keep fresh water available for your dog at camp. Some dogs don't like to drink immediately after exercise and can become dehydrated easily if their owner forgets to provide water after the hike.

Several companies make dog bowls that can fold into a pocket, attach to a backpack, or collapse flat. Make sure to filter any water from streams and lakes to avoid risk of bacterial diseases.

CHOOSING THE RIGHT TENT

Depending on the size of your dog, you're going to want to include it as a person when selecting your tent. If your dog sleeps with you in your bed at home, then you already know how much space it can take up. For example, if you are one person and a dog, then you'll want to look for a two-person tent.

Dogs are known to rip the mesh of tents, so if you think this might be your dog, make sure to clip its nails and get it accustomed to the tent for a few weeks before your first trip. It might be a good idea to carry a repair kit on the first few trips if you have a pawsy pup.

TETHER SYSTEMS

If your dog doesn't already have a solid "place" command, a tether system is a great way to give both of you a little freedom. You can make your own, or Ruffwear makes one called the Knot-a-Hitch.

The concept is that you tie either end between two trees and attach a line on a pulley to your dog. This allows your dog to run around a bit and explore while freeing you to set up the tent or cook without having to constantly monitor its whereabouts.

KEEPING THE TENT CLEAN

Dogs love to get dirty. They play in mud, roll in dead things, and enjoy playing in the water. Bring along a small microfiber towel to wipe off paws before settling in for the night. For especially muddy dogs, dog shower options come in handy.

A shower bag can be hung up to let gravity create the shower stream. Another option is a simple shower cap that can attach to most water bottles. Kurgo is one quality brand to look for.

DON'T FORGET TO CHECK FOR TICKS!

Be aware if you are hiking in areas with ticks and perform multiple checks on your dog. I like to do a once-over right after we finish a hike and then again before bed. This can be a really sweet bonding experience with your dog. Most love tick checks because they are essentially doggy massages!

I also check again in the morning and for several days afterward. Ticks swell up as they fill with blood, so you'll be able to easily notice any that you may have missed during the first several checks.

The easiest way to remove them is with a tick removal device. I have one that looks sort of like a dental tool. It's a stick with a loop made from fishing line and has a slider that can close around the tick. When you have the bug secure, pull while twisting. Make sure you get the head because that is the part that does the damage.

If you do find a tick on your dog, keep it in a small jar filled with rubbing alcohol or store in a zip-top bag and keep in the freezer. Diseases can take time to show symptoms, but you can order a Universal Tick Test and send in the specimen. Test results take from 24 to 72 hours.

BACKPACKING WITH DOGS

If you want a mix of hiking and camping, then backpacking is the way to go! It's a wonderful activity to do with your dog, and it really helps solidify your bond. You'll have to rely on each other. I especially love to take my dog on solo trips. It boosts confidence for me and creates the space for special one-on-one time with my dog.

I recommend going with seasoned friends the first few times. You'll learn immensely from them and will quickly see what you do and don't need to bring. They will also have gear that you don't have that you can share or borrow.

WHAT CAN MY DOG CARRY?

When you bring your dog backpacking, it's not really all that different from packing what you would need for camping and hiking. Depending on their size and weight, dogs may even be able to share the load in their pack.

To ensure proper fit, measure the circumference of your dog's chest and match it to the sizing chart on the product you are considering purchasing. When you have the pack, place the chest strap over your dog's head and lay the pack on over the center of your dog's back. Connect the straps and then tighten for fit. You want to be able to fit two fingers between the straps and your dog's body. Make sure not to keep them too loose, as that can cause chafing.

I also look for packs that have various pockets so I can organize gear and distribute the weight more evenly.

While I've seen suggestions that dogs can carry up to 25 percent of their weight, I max my dogs out at 10 percent. Since they don't carry weight often, I don't want to unexpectedly load them with a heavy backpack. I have Sitka carry his food, water bowl, a thin jacket, and some treats. On the way out, I trade his food for his poop.

If there is a vault toilet where you are backpacking, you can toss your dog's poop (not the bag) down the hatch. Otherwise, bring a few extra zip-top bags and store the poop in there for the return.

Keep an eye out for signs of distress. If it's hot outside, you may need to remove the backpack and carry it yourself. If you notice any limping or altered movement, the fit could be off or the weight could be too much for your dog.

ESSENTIAL ITEMS

I listed all the dog gear that you'll need to bring for a backpacking trip in the checklists, but I wanted to expand on a few items here.

DOG JACKET—You may be surprised how cold your dog might get, even during the summer. The nights can get cold. I once made the mistake of only bringing a rain jacket for my dog on an unexpectedly chilly trip and the poor guy was shivering when we were hanging out at camp during the day. I had to send him into my tent to get under my sleeping bag to stay warm. Now I always bring a warm jacket.

BUG SUIT—These full-body suits look rather silly on dogs, but they'll thank you when it keeps the mosquitoes away. Look for one that goes over the head so that they are as

protected as much as possible. During a different backpacking trip, poor Sitka was so annoyed by the buzzing creatures that he got up, walked to our tent, and stared at me until I let him inside.

DOG BED—Bring a lightweight yet well-padded dog bed so that your dog has a place to lie both during the day and then in your tent at night when you sleep (though if your dog is like mine, it will try and steal your cushy pad instead!).

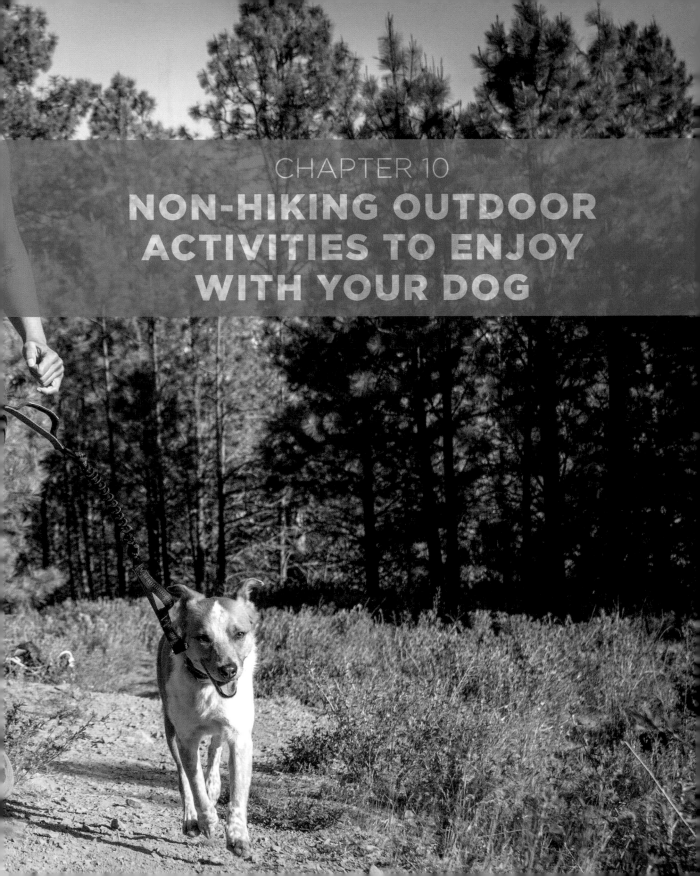

CHAPTER 10

NON-HIKING OUTDOOR ACTIVITIES TO ENJOY WITH YOUR DOG

HIKING ISN'T THE ONLY WAY to enjoy the great outdoors with your pup! I regularly engage in a variety of outdoor activities with my dogs all year-round. Here are a few to try out with your pup.

TRAIL RUNNING

Trail running is pretty much the same as hiking, only you're going at a faster speed. It means that both you and your dog will need to build more cardio strength than for hiking alone. You'll also be going longer distances, often with steeper terrain.

This is my preferred way to enjoy the outdoors with my dogs. I love nothing more than going for a long run in the mountains with my dog by my side. There are even many trail races that allow your dogs to join you!

The longest distance I have run with my dogs is 20 miles, but I have friends whose dogs have joined them for 30-plus-mile runs. As with any endurance effort, it's all about the training. With the right conditioning, your dog should be able to join you for plenty of miles.

GEAR

I carry a trail running–specific backpack for myself. These are lightweight packs that fit water bottles or a hydration bladder, jackets, food, and other small essentials. When you trail run with your dog, you'll also need to plan for space to carry extra water, treats, a water bowl, and poop.

For shorter runs on cooler days, you could have your dog carry a lightweight backpack to store their poop and treats.

Always bring along the 10 Essentials for both you and your pup.

MOUNTAIN BIKING

Jane Patten started mountain biking when she adopted her dog, Moose. He was a natural at the sport, and together they have enjoyed some amazing days on the trails that she will cherish forever.

Mountain biking is a great sport for getting outdoors and exploring trails, and in fact the only way to top it is doing it with your furry best friend. If you ride, you know that feeling

TIPS FOR MOUNTAIN BIKING WITH DOGS
CONTRIBUTED BY JANE PATTEN

WHEN WE ADOPTED MOOSE, we knew he was going to be our adventure buddy, but we didn't have any real expectations for him being a trail dog with the bikes. We wanted to wait until he was fully grown before we took him out riding, so in the meantime we enrolled him in training classes and just got him used to being around bikes in the yard.

After six months, we started taking him out on short little rides to get all of us comfortable riding together. Initially, there was a learning curve teaching him to stay clear of the bike, but after working with him he took to riding fairly quickly. In fact, now Moose loves running down giant rock slabs and hucking off rocks, and he's better than me most of the time! It's apparent he gets as much joy out of riding as we do!

Here are a few tips I've picked up over the years to help make riding with your dog a positive experience.

Know Your Dog's Limits
Every dog is different and not all dogs are cut out to be trail dogs. It's important to know your dog's limits for their health, safety, and enjoyment. Some dogs can easily do 15 miles while others max out at 5, and it's important to remember it's about riding to their level out there not to yours.

Basic Commands
It's important that your dog knows basic commands out on the trail such as recall, sit, and stay. If your dog isn't well trained, it's going to cause a lot of issues not only for you and your dog's riding safety but for other people out on the trail as well.

This also goes for your dog's socialization level. No one wants to come across an aggressive dog out riding. It's up to you to put your dog in situations where it succeeds and has positive experiences. If your dog tends to be reactive or aggressive, think about riding trails that are more remote and less populated.

Building Endurance
After you have basic training commands down, then get your dog comfortable with being around bikes. When first starting out, plan on doing short rides; not

only are you getting your dog comfortable, you're also conditioning it. Would you run 10 miles your first time trail running? Probably not. When starting out, it can be helpful to choose a place with limited distractions.

After you and your dog have had successful short rides, begin to gradually do longer ones. Eventually you'll be able to gauge the sweet spot of what your dog can comfortably handle. It's important to know what your dog's particular limits are, as dogs won't stop and will go longer and farther than they should.

Weather

In addition to what your dog is comfortable with for riding mileage, it's also important to be mindful of heat. In my experience, once temps hit 75°F, Moose really starts to feel the adverse effects of heat. His pace is much slower and he tends to tire out more quickly. If you find your dog doesn't handle heat well, limit your ride length, choose cooler times of day to ride, or take a break from riding and find a water hole.

Be a Good Ambassador

While riding with Moose, I find most people are excited to see him out there; however, not everyone enjoys dogs or are keen about dogs off leash.

Don't hesitate to ask people if they are comfortable having your dog ride with you. Maybe riding with a dog is new and uncomfortable, maybe they're scared of dogs—these are all important questions to ask! Also be aware and respectful of leash laws.

Gear and Accessories

WATER

Riding in an area with some water source like a stream or creek is always ideal for your pup to get a drink or soak in, but this isn't always available. Always ensure you have plenty of water for you and your dog for proper hydration. Training your dog to drink from your Camelbak hose is super convenient, but you may need to bring a collapsible bowl in your pack.

POOP BAGS

Make sure you pick up your dog's waste while out riding. Nothing will anger other trail users more than leaving your dog's poop along the trail.

LEASH

I always make sure I have a small leash in my pack. You never know when you may need one. You may encounter wildlife, horses, hikers, or other dogs out on the trail and you'll need to leash your dog up quickly. There may also be times when you have to ride a section of road.

BELL

Adding a bell to Moose was a game changer for me. When mountain biking you're often focused on the trail ahead, and being preoccupied with where your dog is in relation to your bike can make you lose focus. When Moose wears a bell, I know exactly where he is and I can refocus my attention to the trail ahead. As a bonus, other riders and hikers hear him as well.

TREATS

Just like you, your dog needs trail snacks for fuel. Not only are you burning calories but so is your dog. Treats are also handy if you encounter wildlife or other user groups on the trail to help bring your dog's focus back on you.

HARNESS

I really like having my dog wear some sort of harness on the trail. It's easy to grab him suddenly and control him.

BACKPACK

There are several options out there for dog backpacks. Depending on your dog some may fit better than others. Find one that can hold water bladders. It's also a great way for your dog to carry its own poop bags.

BOOTIES

Every dog is different, and some dogs will be prone to tearing their pads out on the trails. If this is an issue, you may want to look into having your dog wearing booties for protection. You may also want them depending on the terrain you're riding.

OPPOSITE: STEPHANIE CLEMENS, JEN SOTOLONGO

of pure joy mixed with adrenaline. To look down and see your dog smiling back up at you after you both just experienced the same trail is an incredibly special moment that deepens your connection.

Biking with dogs is also a great way to keep them healthy and active.

WATER SPORTS

Paddleboarding, kayaking, and canoeing are all wonderful, low-impact activities to do with your dog. Some dogs will be weirded out by the rocking sensation, so I start by training in the backyard on solid ground, using my favorite command: place!

Get dogs used to getting onto the board or kayak or into the canoe, but make sure to take out all the paddles and other gear you might use on a trip. You want your dog to associate the gear with an outing.

Once your dog has mastered place on the watercraft, wobble the board or boat back and forth to mimic the sensation of being off balance in the water. Next, go to a shore or boat launch and practice in the water.

When your dog has that down, you can set sail! You'll want to strongly enforce that place command on the paddleboard and kayak. If your dog is allowed to move constantly, that will send you off balance and you'll end up in the water.

Make sure that your dog is wearing a fitted life jacket at all times, even if it is a masterful swimmer. Look for one with handles so that you can easily lift your dog onto the vessel if it falls off or goes for a swim.

I use an inflatable paddleboard designed for touring. I can take it pretty much anywhere and it only takes a few minutes to inflate once I arrive at my destination.

BICYCLE TOURING

I mentioned the two-year bike trip across Europe and South America I took with my dog and former partner in the introduction of this book. Like a road trip, only much, much slower, bicycle touring is a wonderful way to travel. It takes you to the places you miss when you travel by car, and I can guarantee that you will attract a lot of attention when you're towing a dog.

THE BIKE TRAILER

We used a Burley Design Tail Wagon for the majority of our trip. Designed specifically for dogs, this trailer is well-designed and rugged, and includes features like mesh paneling to keep your dog cool in hotter weather.

Some dogs will take to the trailer immediately, while others will require an acclimation period. For those who are a bit leery of the new contraption, treat it like you would when you are crate training and use the place command.

Reward your dog for inspecting the trailer, put the brakes on and feed it inside, and allow it to enter on its own. Keep it set up in the house for a period of time so that your dog gets used to it. Next, attach it to your bike and teach your dog how to hop inside. Roll your bike back and forth so it gets used to the sensation of the movement.

When you're ready to pedal, start with very short rides up and down your street. You can leash your pup into the trailer initially, so it doesn't jump out. Do this regularly in the beginning so it learns that it's no big deal.

PLANNING A BIKE TRIP

If you're just starting out as a cyclist and bicycle traveler, I suggest that you pick a popular bike trail that has somewhere to camp along the way. You can do an overnight trip to get a feel for the mode of transportation and identify what gear you might want to leave behind or bring next time.

As you become more confident, you can start to do multiday trips. Look up designated bike routes online, ask bike shops, or talk to the local tourism board for information on cycling.

Determine how many miles you want to ride daily, and make sure that you know where the food, water, and sleep options fall along the way.

Download an offline mapping app for your phone and consider investing in a phone mount for your bike so that you can have your route planned out and your map visible at all times.

BICYCLE TOURING GEAR

Packing for a bicycle tour is a lot like planning for a backpacking trip. The main difference is that you can stop for food along the way, if you are riding through more populated areas. But like backpacking, you're going to want to keep the weight as light as possible.

In addition, you'll want waterproof panniers, head-to-toe rain gear, safety equipment like a helmet and lights, and a spare tire and patch kit.

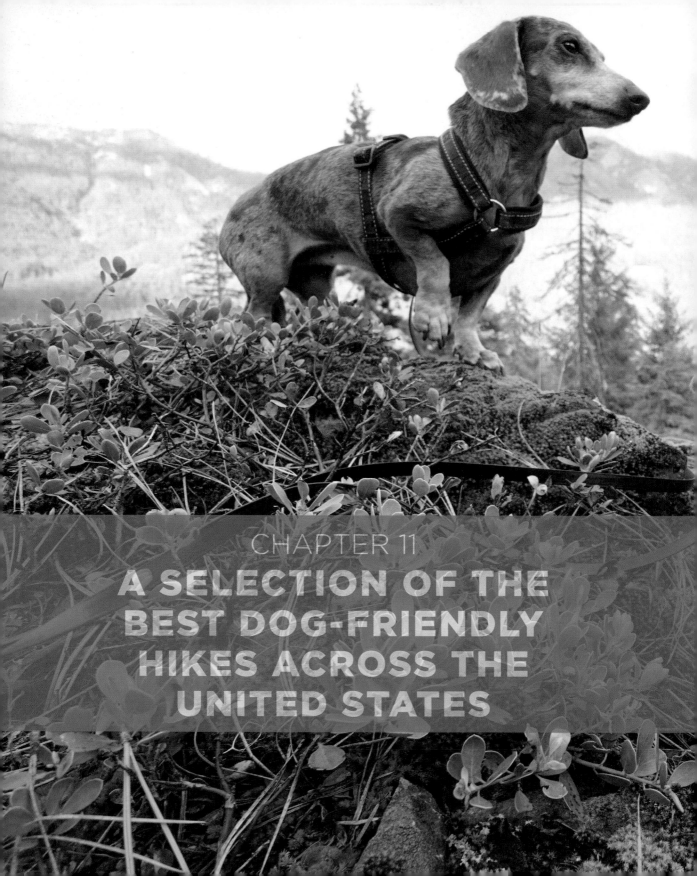

CHAPTER 11

A SELECTION OF THE BEST DOG-FRIENDLY HIKES ACROSS THE UNITED STATES

IT WOULD BE IMPOSSIBLE TO FIT all of the best dog-friendly hikes across the country into the pages of this book. This is the very reason that entire hiking books on single states exist! This country has an expansive array of beautiful hikes, many of which we can enjoy with our dogs.

I know a few regions very well (the Pacific Northwest) and the rest not at all. I included hikes here that I've either done, have wanted to do, or would want to do. This is all based on research and conversations with friends from specific parts of the country.

This selection of hikes includes a variety of short, long, and overnight trips, all of which allow dogs. In states with national parks that allow dogs, I included that national park, since it is such a rare find.

I scoured tourism boards, Reddit threads, hiking apps, and personal blogs to find what I consider some of the best hikes across the United States. I hope that you have the chance to explore some of these with your pup.

WEST COAST

WASHINGTON //
CHAIN LAKES LOOP
GLACIER

Hike overview: Get up close and personal with two of Washington's most prominent peaks: Mount Baker (Koma Kulshan) and Mount Shuksan. Go for a day hike or spend the night at one of the lakes. During the fall, the colors are spectacular.

Distance: 6.5-mile loop, with options for additional distances

Hiking time: 4–6 hours

Difficulty: Moderate

Elevation gain: 1,820 feet

Highest point: 5,400 feet

Trail surface: Singletrack trail

When to go: July to beginning of Oct

Backpackable? Yes

Canine compatibility: Yes, on leash

Fees and permits: Northwest Forest Pass

Trail contact: Mount Baker Ranger District, 810 SR 20, Sedro-Woolley, WA 98284; (360) 856-5700, ext. 515

OREGON // TOM, DICK, AND HARRY MOUNTAIN
GOVERNMENT CAMP

Hike overview: A well-maintained and moderate trail leads to a rocky peak with Mount Hood right smack in view. On a clear day, look for other nearby peaks like Mount Adams and Mount Rainier.

Distance: 3.7–9 miles depending on destination

Hiking time: 3–9 hours

Difficulty: Moderate

Elevation gain: 1,709 feet

Highest point: 4,930 feet

Trail surface: Singletrack trail

When to go: July to beginning of Oct

Backpackable? Yes, camping available at Mirror Lake

Canine compatibility: Yes, on leash

Fees and permits: Northwest Forest Pass

Trail contact: Zigzag Ranger District, 70220 E. Hwy. 26, Zigzag, OR 97049; (503) 622-3191

IDAHO // CHIMNEY ROCK
COOLIN

Hike overview: Hike in the northernmost part of Idaho for a spectacular view of Chimney Rock, a stand-alone 380-foot-tall "lightning rod" carved by glaciers.

Distance: 10.5 miles

Hiking time: 5–7 hours

Difficulty: Moderate

Elevation gain: 2,860 feet

Highest point: 6,755 feet

Trail surface: Singletrack trail

When to go: July to Oct

Backpackable? Yes, if you continue on to Mount Roothan

Canine compatibility: Yes

Fees and permits: None

Trail contact: Priest Lake Ranger District, 32203 Hwy. 57, Priest River, ID 83856; (208) 267-5561

CALIFORNIA // LITTLE LAKE VALLEY TO GEM LAKE

MAMMOTH LAKES & BISHOP (FULL SERVICE), CROWLEY LAKE & TOM'S PLACE (LIMITED SERVICES)

Hike overview: This relatively easy hike enables most able hikers to experience the eastern Sierras without the skills required for other hikes in the range, making this a popular hike. Hike through aspen forests to a chain of lakes with towering peaks as the backdrop.

Distance: 7.2 miles

Hiking time: 5–7 hours

Difficulty: Moderate

Elevation gain: 994 feet

Highest point: 10,943 feet

Trail surface: Singletrack trail

When to go: June to Oct

Backpackable? Yes

Canine compatibility: Yes, on leash

Fees and permits: None for day use, overnight trips require a permit

Trail contact: Inyo National Forest, 351 Pacu Ln., Ste. 200, Bishop, CA 93514; (760) 873-2400

NEVADA // SOUTH OAK CREEK TRAIL

LAS VEGAS

Hike overview: This easy desert hike featuring large red-rock formations makes a perfect day trip from Las Vegas. Though there are shaded spots and a creek on this trail, avoid hiking in the heat of summer. Equestrian traffic is common.

Distance: 5.5 miles

Hiking time: About 3.5 hours

Difficulty: Moderate

Elevation gain: 623 feet

Highest point: 4,178 feet

Trail surface: Singletrack trail, rocky

When to go: Mar to Oct

Backpackable? No

Canine compatibility: Yes

Fees and permits: Red Rock Canyon pass

Trail contact: Red Rock Canyon Visitor Center, 1000 Scenic Loop Dr., Las Vegas, NV 89161; (702) 515-5367

ALASKA // REED LAKES TRAIL

SUTTON

Hike overview: Hike in the shadow of 6,000-foot peaks, alongside a waterfall pouring from a granite ledge and a turquoise mountain lake. You get to climb a boulder field to reach Upper Reed Lake. Keep an eye out for marmots after your food!

Distance: 4.5 miles

Hiking time: 3–4 hours

Difficulty: Moderate

Elevation gain: 2,200 feet

Highest point: 4,250 feet

Trail surface: Singletrack trail, boulder field

When to go: May to Oct

Backpackable? No

Canine compatibility: Yes, on leash

Fees and permits: None

Trail contact: Division of Parks & Outdoor Recreation Atwood Building, 550

ALYSSA SALAVA

W. 7th Ave., Ste. 1380, Anchorage, AK 99501; (907) 269-8700

HAWAII // AIHUALAMA AND NU'UANU LOOP

HONOLULU

Hike overview: Not far from Honolulu, this loop features a waterfall and great bird-watching and flower peeping. It can get muddy after a rainfall, but has great views at the top, and you can go for a dip in the waterfall pool.

Distance: 5.8 miles

Hiking time: 3–4 hours

Difficulty: Moderate

Elevation gain: 1,984 feet

Highest point: 1,850 feet

Trail surface: Singletrack trail, roots

When to go: Year-round

Backpackable? No

Canine compatibility: Yes, on leash

Fees and permits: None

Trail contact: Honolulu Watershed Forest Reserve Kalanimoku Building, 1151 Punchbowl St., Rm. 325, Honolulu, HI 96813; (808) 587-0166

ROCKY MOUNTAIN WEST

COLORADO // ARAPAHOE PASS AND DOROTHY LAKE TRAIL

ELDORA

Hike overview: An easy-to-access hike from Denver and Boulder, Dorothy Lake is one of the most scenic spots in the Indian Peaks Wilderness. Enjoy views of the Indian Peaks all along the way and keep an eye out for Mount Jasper and Mount Neva.

Distance: 7.1 miles

Hiking time: 5–7 hours

Difficulty: Moderate

Elevation gain: 1,942 feet

Highest point: 12,061 feet

Trail surface: Singletrack trail

When to go: July to Sept

Backpackable? Yes

Canine compatibility: Yes

Fees and permits: None

Trail contact: Boulder Ranger District, 2140 Yarmouth Ave., Boulder, CO 80301; (303) 541-2500

MONTANA // EAST ROSEBUD TRAIL TO ELK LAKE

ROSCOE

Hike overview: This family-friendly hike has minimal elevation gain along a well-maintained trail that features a waterfall and a lake. Take a dip in Elk Lake if you feel like braving the chilly waters.

Distance: 6.7 miles

Hiking time: 3–4 hours

Difficulty: Easy

Elevation gain: 807 feet

Highest point: 6,804 feet

Trail surface: Singletrack trail

When to go: May to Oct

Backpackable? Yes

Canine compatibility: Yes, on leash

Fees and permits: None

Trail contact: Custer Gallatin National Forest, 10 E. Babcock Ave., PO Box 130, Bozeman, MT 59711; (406) 587-6701

WYOMING // LOWER GREEN RIVER LAKE LOOP

DUBOIS

Hike overview: This easy hike features a beautiful loop around Green River Lake with Squaretop Mountain as the backdrop. Go prepared to encounter bears. River crossings can be dangerous during snowmelt. Stay at the campground near the lake and bring a paddleboard.

Distance: 6.3 miles

Hiking time: 3–4 hours

Difficulty: Moderate

Elevation gain: 574 feet

Highest point: 8,158 feet

Trail surface: Singletrack trail

When to go: June to Oct

Backpackable? No

Canine compatibility: Yes

Fees and permits: None

Trail contact: Bridger-Teton National Forest, 340 N. Cache, P.O. Box 1888, Jackson, WY 83001; (307) 739-5500

SOUTHWEST

NEW MEXICO // WHITE SANDS NATIONAL PARK

ALAMOGORDO

Hike overview: This national park allows dogs on leash on all trails within the boundary, which is a treat for dog owners who want to see a national park. The Alkali Flat Trail in particular is a 5-mile loop that takes you up and over sand dunes.

Distance: Less than 1 mile–5 miles

Hiking time: 3–4 hours

Difficulty: Moderate

Elevation gain: Varies

Highest point: About 4,000 feet

Trail surface: Sand

When to go: Year-round, though summer can be extremely hot

Backpackable? No

Canine compatibility: Yes

Fees and permits: National park pass

Trail contact: National Park Service, PO Box 1086, Holloman AFB, NM 88330; (575) 479-6124

ARIZONA // HORTON CREEK TRAIL

PAYSON

Hike overview: This mostly shaded hike follows along a creek and features a

waterfall during the right season. Head there early or during the week to avoid crowds.

Distance: 8.5 miles

Hiking time: 6–8 hours

Difficulty: Moderate

Elevation gain: 2,431 feet

Highest point: 6,850 feet

Trail surface: Singletrack trail

When to go: Spring and fall

Backpackable? Yes

Canine compatibility: Yes, on leash

Fees and permits: None

Trail contact: Payson Ranger District, 1009 E. Hwy. 260, Payson, AZ 85541; (928) 474-7900

UTAH // BUCKSKIN GULCH

KANAB

Hike overview: Located inside Paria Canyon, one of the largest slot canyons in the world, Buckskin Gulch is a relatively easy slot canyon experience for those with dogs. Bring plenty of water and a harness to help lift your dog over ladders. Beware of rattlesnakes and flash floods.

Distance: 11.2 miles (5.6 if you bring two cars)

Hiking time: 6–8 hours

Difficulty: Moderate

Elevation gain: 1,246 feet

Highest point: 5,051 feet

Trail surface: Sandstone, sand

When to go: Spring and fall

Backpackable? Yes

Canine compatibility: Yes

Fees and permits: Backpacking permit from BLM if camping overnight, including one for your dog

Trail contact: Kanab Field Office, 669 S. Hwy. 89A, Kanab, UT 84741; (435) 644-1300

MIDWEST

OHIO // MOHICAN TRAIL LOOP
LOUDONVILLE

Hike overview: This lovely trail is accessible all year and especially beautiful in the fall when the trees show off their colors. During the summer months, you can float back down the river with an inner tube to the campground. Mountain bikers also use this trail.

Distance: 6 miles

Hiking time: 3–4 hours

Difficulty: Moderate

Elevation gain: 767 feet

Highest point: 1,245 feet

Trail surface: Singletrack trail

When to go: Year-round

Backpackable? No

Canine compatibility: Yes, on leash

Fees and permits: None

Trail contact: Mohican State Park, 3116 OH 3, Loudonville, OH 44842; (419) 994-5125

MICHIGAN //
MIRROR LAKE TRAIL
ONTONAGON

Hike overview: Starting from popular Lake of the Clouds, follow the trail to

Mirror Lake, where you can find camping among the wooded forest. Mosquitoes can be horrendous in the summer months, and fall is gorgeous with all the changing colors.

Distance: 7.8 miles

Hiking time: 3–4 hours

Difficulty: Moderate

Elevation gain: 1,108 feet

Highest point: 1,654 feet

Trail surface: Singletrack trail, muddy

When to go: Apr to Oct

Backpackable? Yes

Canine compatibility: Yes, on leash

Fees and permits: Yes, make a reservation for backcountry campsites

Trail contact: Porcupine Mountains Wilderness State Park, 3333 Headquarters Rd., Ontonagon, MI 49953; (906) 885-5275

MINNESOTA // HIGH FALLS
AND TWO STEP FALLS
SILVER BAY

Hike overview: Follow the short paved path to a viewpoint of High Falls, the tallest waterfall partially located in Minnesota (the falls shares a border with Canada). During high river flow, High Falls is especially spectacular.

Distance: 1.2 miles

Hiking time: 1–2 hours

Difficulty: Easy

Elevation gain: 65 feet

Highest point: 528 feet

Trail surface: Singletrack trail

When to go: May to Oct

JOANNA LEE

Backpackable? No

Canine compatibility: Yes, on leash

Fees and permits: State park pass

Trail contact: Grand Portage State Park, 9393 E. Hwy. 61, Grand Portage, MN 55605; (218) 475-2360

SOUTH DAKOTA //
SAINT ELMO PEAK

CUSTER

Hike overview: This short hike is perfect for a sunset picnic. The rock outcropping at the top makes the ideal perch to enjoy a meal and look out over the Black Hills National Forest. The hike is steep, but worth the calf pain!

Distance: 1.8 miles

Hiking time: 2–3 hours

Difficulty: Difficult

Elevation gain: 1,190 feet

Highest point: 6,458 feet

Trail surface: Singletrack trail, slate rock

When to go: Year-round

Backpackable? No

Canine compatibility: Yes

Fees and permits: Black Hills Forest Annual Recreation Pass

Trail contact: Black Hills National Forest, 1019 N. 5th St. Custer, SD 57730; (605) 673-9200

WISCONSIN //
MEYERS BEACH SEA CAVE

BAYFIELD

Hike overview: While most visitors choose to view the Apostle Island Caves via kayak, a hike offers a perspective from above. The trail begins along a boardwalk before evolving into a dirt path with rolling hills.

Distance: 4.6 miles

Hiking time: 2–3 hours

Difficulty: Moderate

Elevation gain: 269 feet

Highest point: 680 feet

Trail surface: Boardwalk, singletrack trail

When to go: Year-round

Backpackable? No

Canine compatibility: Yes, on leash

Fees and permits: Parking fee

Trail contact: Apostle Island National Lakeshore, 412 Washington Ave., Bayfield, WI 54814; (715) 779-3397

MISSOURI //
CAVE SPRING LOOP

SALEM

Hike overview: Visit one of the largest springs in Missouri and peek into a cave located at the base of a bluff that pours 32 million gallons of water into the Current River daily. You can also paddle on the river to the cave.

Distance: 4.8 miles

Hiking time: 2–3 hours

Difficulty: Moderate

Elevation gain: 688 feet

Highest point: 1,008 feet

Trail surface: Singletrack trail

When to go: Year-round

Backpackable? No

Canine compatibility: Yes, on leash

Fees and permits: None

Trail contact: Kansas City Parks & Rec, PO Box 490, Van Buren, MO 63965; (573) 323-4236

INDIANA //
SYCAMORE LOOP TRAIL
BLOOMINGTON

Hike overview: If you're looking for an easy overnight backpacking excursion, Sycamore Loop in Hoosier National Forest is a great choice. Spring and summer bring beautiful wildflowers, while the fall features a rainbow of leaves. There are several camping spots along the loop.

Distance: 6.4 miles

Hiking time: 2–3 hours

Difficulty: Moderate

Elevation gain: 482 feet

Highest point: 896 feet

Trail surface: Singletrack trail

When to go: Year-round

Backpackable? Yes

Canine compatibility: Yes, on leash

Fees and permits: None

Trail contact: Hoosier National Forest, 811 Constitution Ave., Bedford, IN 47421; (812) 275-5987

ILLINOIS // DELLS CANYON
AND BLUFF TRAIL
OGLESBY

Hike overview: This hike in Matthiessen State Park follows a trail in and out of a canyon and features a river and a beautiful waterfall with a swimming area.

Distance: 2 miles

Hiking time: 1–2 hours

Difficulty: Moderate

Elevation gain: 206 feet

Highest point: 638 feet

Trail surface: Singletrack trail

When to go: Year-round

Backpackable? No

Canine compatibility: Yes, on leash

Fees and permits: None

Trail contact: Matthiessen State Park, Box 509, Utica, IL 61373; (815) 667-4868

IOWA // SQUIRE SHORE,
WEASEL RUN, MUSHROOM
FOREST TRAIL
NORTH LIBERTY

Hike overview: This is a great family-friendly hike that features a well-maintained trail with a perfect picnicking area located on Coralville Lake, a large man-made reservoir. The park features over 25 miles of trails, a boat launch, and a campground.

Distance: 5 miles

Hiking time: 2–3 hours

Difficulty: Moderate

Elevation gain: 364 feet

Highest point: 810 feet

Trail surface: Singletrack trail

When to go: Year-round

Backpackable? No, but there is a campground

Canine compatibility: Yes, on leash

Fees and permits: None

Trail contact: Coralville Lake Project Office, 2850 Prairie du Chien Rd. NE, Iowa City, IA 52240; (319) 338-3543

NORTH DAKOTA // LONG X TO MAAH DAAH HEY LOOP

WATFORD CITY

Hike overview: This seldom-used trail meanders through various ecosystems and parallels the Little Missouri River, following the original route of the early cattle drivers. Once you leave the trees, enjoy the views of the badlands and the river.

Distance: 5.8 miles

Hiking time: 2–3 hours

Difficulty: Moderate

Elevation gain: 1,122 feet

Highest point: 2,566 feet

Trail surface: Singletrack trail

When to go: Year-round

Backpackable? Yes

Canine compatibility: Yes, on leash

Fees and permits: None

Trail contact: McKenzie Ranger District, 1905 S. Main St., Watford City, ND 58854; (701) 842-8500

NEBRASKA // LOVER'S LEAP BUTTE

CRAWFORD

Hike overview: Located inside Nebraska's largest state park, you'll find several unique geological features like steep buttes and small peaks.

Distance: 6.5 miles

Hiking time: 3–4 hours

Difficulty: Moderate

Elevation gain: 1,289 feet

Highest point: 4,355 feet

Trail surface: Singletrack trail

When to go: May to Oct

Backpackable? No

Canine compatibility: Yes, on leash

Fees and permits: Yes

Trail contact: Pine Ridge Ranger District, 125 N. Main St., Chadron, NE 69337; (308) 432-0300

KANSAS // MANHATTAN RIVER TRAIL

MANHATTAN

Hike overview: This trail follows the west bank of the Blue River and connects to the other two waterways that flow through the city of Manhattan. Keep an eye out for the old rusty car that makes for a good photo op.

Distance: 5.4 miles

Hiking time: 3–4 hours

Difficulty: Easy

Elevation gain: 95 feet

Highest point: 1,015 feet

Trail surface: Singletrack trail

When to go: Mar to Oct

Backpackable? No

Canine compatibility: Yes, on leash

Fees and permits: None

Trail contact: Manhattan Parks and Rec, 1101 Poyntz Ave., Manhattan, KS 66502; (785) 587-2757

NEW ENGLAND

VERMONT // MOUNT PISGAH

ORLEANS

Hike overview: Enjoy overlooks of Lake Willoughby, the Passumpsic Valley, and

the White Mountains from several viewpoints on the way to the top of Mount Pisgah.

Distance: 4.1 miles

Hiking time: 2–3 hours

Difficulty: Moderate

Elevation gain: 1,653 feet

Highest point: 2,786 feet

Trail surface: Singletrack trail, ladders, rocks

When to go: Mar to Oct

Backpackable? No

Canine compatibility: Yes, on leash

Fees and permits: None

Trail contact: Vermont Department of Forests, Parks and Recreation, District 5: St. Johnsbury District, 374 Emerson Falls Rd., Ste. 4, St. Johnsbury, VT 05819; (802) 751-0110

NEW HAMPSHIRE // CHAMPNEY BROOK TRAIL TO MOUNT CHOCORUA

ALBANY

Hike overview: This is one of the most popular hikes in the White Mountains and for good reason. The hike offers beautiful views, and the waterfall along the way gives your pup a spot to cool off on a warm day.

Distance: 7.4 miles

Hiking time: 4–6 hours

Difficulty: Moderate

Elevation gain: 2,244 feet

Highest point: 3,500 feet

Trail surface: Singletrack trail

When to go: Mar to Oct

Backpackable? Yes, only at Camp Penacook and Jim Liberty Cabin

Canine compatibility: Yes, on leash

Fees and permits: White Mountain National Forest recreation pass

Trail contact: Saco Ranger District, 33 Kancamagus Hwy., Conway, NH 03818; (603) 447-5448

MAINE // PENOBSCOT AND SARGENT MOUNTAIN LOOP

BAR HARBOR

Hike overview: Traverse with unobstructed views across two of the highest peaks on Mount Desert Island in dog-friendly Acadia National Park. Arrive early to avoid crowds, and keep in mind that the Jordan Cliffs Trail may be closed during the summer months due to nesting peregrine falcons.

Distance: 5.2 miles

Hiking time: About 3 hours

Difficulty: Moderate

Elevation gain: 1,259 feet

Highest point: 1,375 feet

Trail surface: Singletrack trail, rocks

When to go: Mar to Oct

Backpackable? No

Canine compatibility: Yes, on leash

Fees and permits: National park pass

Trail contact: Acadia National Park, PO Box 177, Bar Harbor, ME 04609; (207) 288-3338

MASSACHUSETTS // KEYSTONE ARCH BRIDGES TRAIL

CHESTER

Hike overview: Go back to the past by hiking along the former railway system that connected eastern Massachusetts with Albany, New York. The stone arch bridges were constructed in 1840 and offer an easy hike with river access and beautiful fall colors.

Distance: 5 miles

Hiking time: About 3 hours

Difficulty: Moderate

Elevation gain: 538 feet

Highest point: 904 feet

Trail surface: Wide gravel path

When to go: Mar to Oct

Backpackable? No

Canine compatibility: Yes, on leash

Fees and permits: None

Trail contact: Friends of the Keystone Arches, Inc., PO Box 276, Huntington, MA 01050

CONNECTICUT // CAMPBELL FALLS

NORFOLK

Hike overview: Hike across state lines on this short waterfall jaunt. Suitable for the whole family, the Campbell Falls hike takes visitors through a gorge leading to a 50-foot waterfall.

Distance: 1.4 miles

Hiking time: 1–2 hours

Difficulty: Easy

Elevation gain: 187 feet

Highest point: 1,135 feet

Trail surface: Singletrack trail

When to go: Year-round

Backpackable? No

Canine compatibility: Yes, on leash

Fees and permits: None

Trail contact: Campbell Falls State Park Reserve, c/o Burr Pond State Park, 385 Burr Mountain Rd., Torrington, CT 06790; (860) 482-1817

RHODE ISLAND //
BLACK POINT TRAIL
NARRAGANSETT

Hike overview: This short ocean trail features sandy beaches, old ruins, woods, and rocky cliffs. You can step off the path and climb among the bluffs to take in the ocean views and search for life in the tidal pools.

Distance: 1.4 miles

Hiking time: 1–2 hours

Difficulty: Easy

Elevation gain: 59 feet

Highest point: 51 feet

Trail surface: Rocks, dirt paths, sand

When to go: Year-round

Backpackable? No

Canine compatibility: Yes, on leash

Fees and permits: None

Trail contact: Rhode Island Department of Environmental Management, 235 Promenade St., Providence, RI 02908; (401) 222-4700

MID-ATLANTIC
NEW YORK // GIANT LEDGE AND PANTHER MOUNTAIN
BIG INDIAN

Hike overview: One of the most popular hikes in the Catskills, and one of the Catskills 35ers, Giant Ledge and Panther Mountain's top offers five ledges to enjoy a view of the mountains. Even on a busy day, you should be able to find a secluded spot to take in the scenery.

Distance: 6.3 miles

Hiking time: 4–5 hours

Difficulty: Moderate

Elevation gain: 1,981 feet

Highest point: 3,721 feet

Trail surface: Singletrack trail, rocks, scrambling

When to go: Year-round

Backpackable? Yes

Canine compatibility: Yes

Fees and permits: None

Trail contact: NYSDEC, 21 S. Putt Corners Rd., New Paltz, NY 12561; (845) 256-3054

PENNSYLVANIA //
HORNBECKS CREEK (INDIAN LADDERS)
DINGMANS FERRY

Hike overview: A relatively unknown trail located in the Poconos Mountains, Hornbecks Creek features three waterfalls along the old roadbed trail. Keep an eye out for the unassuming parking area at the trailhead.

Distance: 2.4 miles

Hiking time: 2–3 hours

Difficulty: Moderate

Elevation gain: 469 feet

Highest point: 832 feet

Trail surface: Singletrack trail, scrambling

When to go: Mar to Nov

Backpackable? No

Canine compatibility: Yes, on leash

Fees and permits: None

Trail contact: National Park Service, 1978 River Rd., Bushkill, PA 18324; (570) 426-2452

NEW JERSEY // MOUNT TAMMANY

WARREN

Hike overview: This steep and popular hike in the Delaware Water Gap is well worth the views and potential crowds. Dogs will likely have an easier time navigating up the Red Dot Trail and down the Blue Dot, due to rock scrambles.

Distance: 3.8 miles

Hiking time: 2–3 hours

Difficulty: Moderate to difficult

Elevation gain: 1,213 feet

Highest point: 1,513 feet

Trail surface: Singletrack trail, boulder fields

When to go: Year-round

Backpackable? No

Canine compatibility: Yes

Fees and permits: Parking pass

Trail contact: Delaware Water Gap National Recreation Area, 1978 River Rd., Bushkill, PA 18324; (570) 426-2452

DELAWARE // GORDON'S POND TRAIL

LEWES

Hike overview: Walk through a 900-acre salt lagoon on this easy excursion located in Cape Henlopen State Park that features maritime forest, marshlands, and sand dunes. Keep an eye out for ospreys and bald eagles that nest in the trees along the path.

Distance: 5.2 miles

Hiking time: 2–3 hours

Difficulty: Easy

Elevation gain: 42 feet

Highest point: 22 feet

Trail surface: Wide dirt path, gravel road, fields, beach

When to go: Year-round

Backpackable? No, but you can camp in the state park

Canine compatibility: Yes, on leash

Fees and permits: Yes

Trail contact: Cape Henlopen State Park, 15099 Cape Henlopen Dr., Lewes, DE 19958; (302) 645-2103

MARYLAND // WOLF ROCK AND CHIMNEY ROCK LOOP

THURMONT

Hike overview: This short but somewhat strenuous hike leads to two rock formations called Chimney Rock and Wolf Rock, lovely perches on which to enjoy a lunch and take in the scenery. Users have reported that the trail is not marked well, so be sure to bring an offline map of the region.

Distance: 3.2 miles

ELLEN REMPEL

Hiking time: 2–3 hours

Difficulty: Moderate

Elevation gain: 790 feet

Highest point: 1,515 feet

Trail surface: Singletrack trail, rocks

When to go: Year-round

Backpackable? No, but you can camp in the state park

Canine compatibility: Yes, on leash

Fees and permits: None

Trail contact: Catoctin Mountain Park, 6602 Foxville Rd., Thurmont, MD 21788; (301) 663-9388

APPALACHIA/ SOUTHEAST

NORTH CAROLINA // TABLE ROCK LOOP FROM SPENCE RIDGE TRAIL

MORGANTON

Hike overview: Take in the views from the top of Table Rock Mountain in North Carolina's Linville Gorge, which are especially gorgeous during the fall. This short but steep hike is worth the effort, and there are some campsites near the parking lot if you want to get an early start. If you feel ambitious, hike nearby Hawksbill Mountain on the same day!

Distance: 3.3 miles

Hiking time: 2–3 hours

Difficulty: Difficult

Elevation gain: 1,302 feet

Highest point: 3,937 feet

Trail surface: Singletrack trail

When to go: Apr to Dec

Backpackable? No

Canine compatibility: Yes, on leash

Fees and permits: Permits required for camping

Trail contact: Grandfather Ranger District Office, 109 E. Lawing Dr., Nebo, NC 28761; (828) 652-2144

VIRGINIA // CRESCENT ROCK VIA APPALACHIAN TRAIL

SYRIA

Hike overview: Shenandoah National Park is one of the few in the United States that welcomes dogs with liberty. Only about 20 of the 500 miles of trails do not permit dogs. This short but sweet hike features a scenic view over the park, as well as a small waterfall and river. There are plenty of options to continue farther if desired.

Distance: 0.9 mile

Hiking time: About 1 hour

Difficulty: Moderate

Elevation gain: 124 feet

Highest point: 3,555 feet

Trail surface: Singletrack trail

When to go: Mar to Sept

Backpackable? No

Canine compatibility: Yes, on leash

Fees and permits: National park pass

Trail contact: Shenandoah National Park, 3655 US 211, East Luray, VA 22835; (540) 999-3500

WEST VIRGINIA //
GLADE CREEK
BECKLEY

Hike overview: Head out for a long day hike or overnight, or choose your own distance on this out-and-back trail in the famous New River Gorge National River. Just a mile into the hike, you come across a beautiful emerald-green swimming hole and waterfall. This hike is great for a hot summer day with the river along the way to keep you and your dog cool.

Distance: 12 miles

Hiking time: Long day hike or overnight backpack

Difficulty: Moderate

Elevation gain: 1,394 feet

Highest point: 2,059 feet

Trail surface: Singletrack trail, river crossings, rocky

When to go: Mar to Nov

Backpackable? Yes

Canine compatibility: Yes, on leash

Fees and permits: None

Trail contact: National Park Service, PO Box 246, 104 Main St., Glen Jean, WV 25846; (304) 465-0508

KENTUCKY //
SWIFT CAMP CREEK
PINE RIDGE

Hike overview: This special area of Kentucky is located in a unique setting that features sandstone arches, waterfalls, cliffsides, and more. This long day hike or overnight trek is a little off the beaten path and sees fewer visitors compared to nearby trails.

Distance: 13.5 miles

Hiking time: Long day hike or overnight backpack

Difficulty: Moderate to difficult

Elevation gain: 2,516 feet

Highest point: 1,173 feet

Trail surface: Singletrack trail, rocks

When to go: Year-round

Backpackable? Yes

Canine compatibility: Yes, on leash

Fees and permits: Permit required

Trail contact: Daniel Boone National Forest, 1700 Bypass Rd., Winchester, KY 40391; (859) 745-3100

TENNESSEE // JONES FALLS
ROAN MOUNTAIN

Hike overview: This out-and-back trail features a beautiful waterfall that is great to visit in all seasons. Cool off in the water during the summer and head there in the winter to see the falls frozen over. If you want to add more miles, just turn off onto the Appalachian Trail. When it's really hot, make sure to head to nearby Elk Falls, just over the state border in North Carolina, to take a dip below a 50-foot waterfall.

Distance: 5.3 miles

Hiking time: 2–3 hours

Difficulty: Moderate

Elevation gain: 972 feet

Highest point: 3,138 feet

Trail surface: Singletrack trail, gravel road

When to go: Mar to Oct

Backpackable? Yes, if you continue to the AT

Canine compatibility: Yes, on leash

Fees and permits: None

Trail contact: Pisgah National Forest Supervisor's Office, 2800 Ocoee St. N., Cleveland, TN 37312; (423) 476-9700

THE SOUTH

SOUTH CAROLINA // RAINBOW FALLS

CLEVELAND

Hike overview: Water plunges over a 100-foot granite wall on this must-do hike. The trail follows a river, starting off with an easy traverse before hitting a steep section with granite and wood steps to climb.

Distance: 4.3 miles

Hiking time: 2–3 hours

Difficulty: Moderate

Elevation gain: 1,207 feet

Highest point: 2,534 feet

Trail surface: Singletrack trail, granite, rocky slopes

When to go: Year-round

Backpackable? No

Canine compatibility: Yes, on leash

Fees and permits: Yes

Trail contact: South Carolina State Parks, 1205 Pendleton St., Ste. 201, Columbia, SC 29201; (803) 734-1700

GEORGIA // SPRINGER MOUNTAIN

DAHLONEGA

Hike overview: Springer Mountain kicks off the start of the Appalachian Trail, making this a popular hiking destination. Overlooking the Blue Ridge Mountains,

this hike is especially beautiful in the fall and winter.

Distance: 10 miles

Hiking time: 5–7 hours

Difficulty: Moderate

Elevation gain: 1,860 feet

Highest point: 3,727 feet

Trail surface: Singletrack trail, muddy

When to go: Year-round

Backpackable? Yes

Canine compatibility: Yes

Fees and permits: None

Trail contact: Chattahoochee-Oconee National Forest Supervisor's Office, 1755 Cleveland Hwy., Gainesville, GA 30501; (770) 297-3000

ARKANSAS // TWIN FALLS TRAIL

WITTS SPRINGS

Hike overview: Twin Falls is one of Arkansas's gems and most scenic waterfalls. The silty blue water will make you think you're at an alpine lake. Bring water shoes and trekking poles, as there are several creek crossings, which can be strong during high water flow.

Distance: 5.1 miles

Hiking time: 2–3 hours

Difficulty: Moderate

Elevation gain: 449 feet

Highest point: 1,193 feet

Trail surface: Singletrack trail, rocks

When to go: Year-round, but best from Nov to May

Backpackable? No, but there is a campground near the trailhead

Canine compatibility: Yes, on leash

Fees and permits: None

Trail contact: Ozark-St. Francis National Forest Supervisor's Office, 605 W. Main, Russellville, AR 72801; (479) 964-7200

ALABAMA // SOUGAHOAGDEE FALLS

HOUSTON

Hike overview: Located in a remote part of the Bankhead National Forest, Sougahoagdee Falls is a bit of an adventure. The trail is mostly well marked and easy to follow, just make sure to always follow the creek. Keep an eye out for side trails leading to other waterfalls.

Distance: 4 miles

Hiking time: 1–2 hours

Difficulty: Easy

Elevation gain: 436 feet

Highest point: 656 feet

Trail surface: Singletrack trail

When to go: Year-round

Backpackable? No, but there is a campground near the trailhead

Canine compatibility: Yes, on leash

Fees and permits: Yes

Trail contact: Bankhead National Forest, 1070 Hwy. 33, Double Springs, AL 35553; (205) 471-7724

FLORIDA // ST. FRANCIS TRAIL

RIVER FOREST

Hike overview: A town used to claim the land that this trail now traverses. Freezing weather, flooding, and the introduction of railroads led to the end of the town. Hunting is popular here during the holiday season, so make sure your dog is wearing an orange vest.

Distance: 7.8 miles

Hiking time: 3–5 hours

Difficulty: Easy

Elevation gain: 72 feet

Highest point: 33 feet

Trail surface: Singletrack trail

When to go: Year-round, but best in cooler, drier months

Backpackable? No, but there is camping nearby

Canine compatibility: Yes, on leash

Fees and permits: Yes

Trail contact: National Forests in Florida, 325 John Knox Rd., Ste. F-100, Tallahassee, FL 32303; (850) 523-8500

MISSISSIPPI // RICHARDSON CREEK TRAIL

ROXIE

Hike overview: Over 20 miles of trail wind through the Homochitto National Forest with plenty of camping at nearby Clear Springs Park. There are many intersecting trails, so bringing an offline map will keep you on track.

Distance: 8 miles

Hiking time: 3–5 hours

Difficulty: Moderate

Elevation gain: 800 feet

Highest point: 404 feet

Trail surface: Singletrack trail

When to go: Year-round

Backpackable? Yes

Canine compatibility: Yes, on leash

Fees and permits: Yes

Trail contact: Homochitto National Forest, 1200 Hwy. 184, East Meadville, MS 39653; (601) 384-5876

LOUISIANA // LONGLEAF VISTA INTERPRETIVE TRAIL

GORUM

Hike overview: This interesting loop features some of the most unique scenery in the state as it travels through a variety of forest settings, including meadows, mesas, creeks, and stands of longleaf pines.

Distance: 1.4 miles

Hiking time: 1–2 hours

Difficulty: Easy

Elevation gain: 164 feet

Highest point: 308 feet

Trail surface: Singletrack trail, stairs

When to go: Year-round

Backpackable? No

Canine compatibility: Yes, on leash

Fees and permits: Yes

Trail contact: Kisatchie Ranger District, 229 Dogwood Park Rd., Provencal, LA 71468; (318) 472-1840

OKLAHOMA // CATHEDRAL MOUNTAIN MESA TRAIL

FAIRVIEW

Hike overview: Located in Gloss Mountain State Park, the Cathedral Mountain hike is a unique experience. The mountains have a high selenite content that makes the scenery appear shiny. The view from the top of the mesa shows off the valley below and Lone Peak Mountain.

Distance: 1.5 miles

Hiking time: 1–2 hours

Difficulty: Moderate

Elevation gain: 201 feet

Highest point: 1,558 feet

Trail surface: Singletrack trail

When to go: Year-round, very hot in summer

Backpackable? No

Canine compatibility: Yes, on leash

Fees and permits: None

Trail contact: Gloss Mountain State Park, north of Fairview off Hwy 412, Fairview, OK 73737; (580) 227-2512

TEXAS // INKS LAKE DEVILS BACKBONE

BURNET

Hike overview: If you're looking for an easy hike with a swimming area on a hot day, this is a great option. Inks Lake includes a few easy creek crossings, rocky scrambles, and a spot to cool off when the temperature soars.

Distance: 3.4 miles

Hiking time: 2–3 hours

Difficulty: Moderate

Elevation gain: 190 feet

Highest point: 1,000 feet

Trail surface: Dirt, boulders, stream crossings

When to go: Year-round

Backpackable? No

Canine compatibility: Yes, on leash

Fees and permits: Texas State Park pass

Trail contact: Inks Lake State Park, 3630 Park Rd. 4 W., Burnet, TX 78611; (512) 793-2223

GEAR GUIDE

CONTRIBUTED BY KATHERINE TAYLOR

HIKING WITH YOUR DOG CAN BE as simple as grabbing any leash, collar, and water bowl (don't forget the poop bags!), but more specialized gear can make it more enjoyable, and safer to venture out a little farther.

LEASHES

There are plenty of innovative designs that can make your hike easier:

> If you hike in wet or muddy conditions, coated biothane webbing cleans up easily.

> For on-leash hikes, consider a hands-free waist leash. Some come with adjustability or built-in elastic for comfort. Euro leads (with a snap on each end) offer multiple configurations including waist leash and ability to walk two dogs. If you'll be running, take a look at skijoring and canicross belts for better support and comfort.

> When hiking in an off-leash area, a short, waist-sized leash (like the Ruffwear Ridgeline or a custom leash) can be convenient since it can be worn as a belt when not in use.

> A traffic tab clipped to the harness or a collar leash like the Ruffwear Quick Draw or Rad Dog Release N' Run makes your medium to large off-leash dog easier to grab at quick notice (these are too big for small dogs).

HARNESSES

Look for a comfortable fit that doesn't shift around or chafe between the front legs or behind the armpits. Avoid harnesses with a band that cuts horizontally across the shoulders in front (this limits range of motion), and make sure there is plenty of clearance for the neck and throat. Ill-fitting harnesses will fit either too loosely or too tightly and will not stay in place. You want to be able to insert two fingers between the straps and your dog's body.

Any well-fitting harness will work, but there are a couple of specialty options for more serious hiking:

> Sturdy assistance harnesses feature a handle at the middle of the back and are great for helping dogs over obstacles. These harnesses usually have two belly straps and cover a lot of the body. The Ruffwear Webmaster is a popular option; Hurtta makes its Trail Harness, and Groundbird Gear makes custom-fit breathable harnesses with full belly support (with optional backpacks).

> For backpacking or longer hikes, healthy dogs can wear backpacks to help carry their own snacks and essentials. Look for a backpack that fits close to the body, balances well, and has an appropriate capacity for your dog's build. Be sure to weigh out gear for your dog's safety.

WATER BOWLS

Anything will work (even your cupped palm if your dog is willing), but there are a few unique options:

> If you'll be feeding your dog on the trail, screw-top silicone bowls can carry the food in and keep your pack clean on the way out. I like the Sea to Summit X-Seal line.

> If you're trail running or packing light, a super packable fabric bowl is the way to go. I find I offer water more often if the bowl is handy in my pocket. I use the Ruffwear Trail Runner, and I've heard good things about the Rad Dog and Wildebeest Montara bowls.

Any time you're venturing farther from civilization, make sure to bring a first-aid kit with necessities for your dog as well as yourself. Look for a compact design with just the items you need and a lightweight, functional case, or you'll find yourself leaving it at home.

DOG BOOTIES

For rough terrain, snow, ice, or in case of injury, consider carrying a set of dog boots. Pawz balloon boots are a good emergency option that packs small, but they don't last long. For small dogs, flexible fabric booties tend to work better than anything with a sole, since they allow small paws to grip the ground through the boot. For larger dogs, rubber-soled boots will last longer but take more getting used to, so prep ahead of time! Snug-fitting socks or boot liners underneath can help prevent blisters and chafing on short-haired dogs.

PACKING LISTS

I LIKE TO KEEP BINS DEDICATED TO CAMPING GEAR and dog gear ready to transfer to the car on a moment's notice. It means that I tend to forget fewer essentials and I can just up and go on a whim.

Of course, there will be seasonal and food needs that you have to consider. I bring different gear for car camping versus backpacking, but much of it is the same. The lists below should serve as a guide for your own adventures. You'll learn what your own essentials are the more you hit the trails.

Winter Hiking
DOG
- ○ Rain jacket
- ○ Water
- ○ Collapsible bowl
- ○ Dog treat pouch
- ○ Treats
- ○ First-aid kit
- ○ Dog goggles
- ○ Winter jacket
- ○ Booties
- ○ Paw wax
- ○ Towel (for car)
- ○ Poop bags

HUMAN
- ○ Headlamp
- ○ Gloves
- ○ Snowshoes or microspikes
- ○ Gaiters or snow pants
- ○ Beanie
- ○ Merino wool baselayer
- ○ Puffy coat
- ○ Sunglasses
- ○ Merino wool socks
- ○ Fully charged phone
- ○ Printed or offline map
- ○ Waterproof hiking boots
- ○ Neck gaiter or scarf
- ○ Waterproof jacket
- ○ Sunblock
- ○ Water
- ○ Snacks
- ○ Camera + extra batteries

Summer Hiking
DOG
- ○ Cooling vest
- ○ Extra water
- ○ Collapsible bowl
- ○ Dog treat pouch
- ○ Treats
- ○ First-aid kit
- ○ Dog goggles

- Towel (for car)
- Booties
- Poop bags

HUMAN
- Headlamp
- Sunglasses
- Sunblock
- Hiking boots
- Hat
- Bug spray
- Water
- Snacks
- Camera
- Fully charged phone
- Long-sleeve layer
- Rain jacket

Backpacking
DOG
- Cooling vest (if hot or on exposed trail)
- Water
- Collapsible bowl
- Dog treat pouch
- Treats
- First-aid kit
- Dog goggles
- Towel (for car)
- Backpack
- Measured food
- Dog bed

- Small microfiber towel
- Warm jacket (for evening)
- Pet-safe bug spray or bandana with insect repellent
- Poop bags
- Booties

HUMAN
- Headlamp
- Sunglasses
- Sunblock
- Hiking boots
- Extra layers
- Rain jacket
- Puffy coat
- Extra batteries
- Portable battery charger
- Printed or offline map
- Sleeping bag
- Sleeping bag liner
- Tent
- Sleeping pad
- Pillow
- Food
- Bear bag or critter-proof bag
- Bug spray
- Hat
- Fully charged phone
- Thin paracord
- Stove
- Matches
- Pot or pan

- Water filter
- Dish soap + sponge
- Toiletries
- Zip-top bags of varying sizes
- Stove fuel
- Dry bags
- Hand sanitizer
- Beanie
- Camera + extra batteries
- Gloves
- Small microfiber towel

Car Camping
DOG
- Cooling vest
- Water
- Collapsible bowl
- Dog treat pouch
- Treats
- First-aid kit
- Dog goggles
- Towel
- Dog bed
- Warm jacket
- Tether
- Dog food
- Toys
- Pet-safe bug spray or bandana with insect repellent

HUMAN
- Headlamp
- Sunglasses
- Sunblock
- Hiking boots
- Sandals/flip-flops
- Sleeping bag
- Tent
- Sleeping pad
- Sleeping bag liner
- Lantern
- Camp stove
- Stove fuel
- Matches/lighter
- Food
- Cooler
- Utensils + plates
- Spices
- Cooking utensils
- Pots + pans
- Camp chair
- Camp table (if not camping at an established site)
- Gloves
- Beanie
- Bug spray
- Beverages
- Camp sink
- Dish soap + sponge
- Hand sanitizer
- Dishtowels
- Microfiber towel
- Pillow
- Blanket

ACKNOWLEDGMENTS

TO MY EDITOR, KATIE O'DELL, who somehow found me on social media and reached out asking if I would be interested in writing a book about hiking with dogs. I missed her first email and, thankfully, she followed up. Thank you for believing that I was the right person to write this book.

To my unofficial editors, Jenna Hlady and my dog trainer, Ruben Montes. Thank you both for jumping without hesitation on my last-minute request to go over the dog behavior and training sections of this book. You provided important notes and guidance for these sections, and I thank you for your honesty and the time spent helping me out where I was stuck.

To my parents, who have always supported my adventures and my dreams, no matter how seemingly crazy and far away they may be, and who have often followed my dog and me around the world (lucky them!). Thank you for welcoming my dogs and me into your home when I'm in between adventures.

To my contributors: Amanda Davis, Dawn Mellon, Joanna Lee, Amber Pitcher, Jane Patten, Katherine Taylor, Rory Riley Topping, Jessica Williams, and Hannah Zululeta. I am beyond grateful for your contributions to this book, for sharing your experiences and expertise, and for being exemplary members of the dog community. I met every single one of you on Instagram and have had the pleasure of meeting many of you and your dogs in person. I hope to do the same with those of you I have yet to meet.

To all my blog readers, friends, and my beloved Instagram community: I would not be writing this book if it were not for your devotion and interest in what I have to say about dogs. I started Long Haul Trekkers to document our bicycle tour, and it evolved into an incredible network that has provided invaluable information, inspiration, and friendship since 2015. I had no idea that I would develop such a wonderful community and build a career just by posting photos of and writing about my dogs.

And finally, to Sitka, my handsome little fox who will never read this, because he is a dog. Thank you for being up for all my adventures and for trusting me to lead you through the life we share together. I have plenty of shenanigans planned for us, Sweet Boy.

CONTRIBUTOR BIOS

AMANDA DAVIS lives in Washington with her rescued pit bull, Lani, whom she adopted from Seattle Humane in 2012. They enjoy hiking, camping, backpacking, swimming, snuggling, and, yes, even long walks on the beach! She uses her social media account for all things dog training, proper trail manners, Leave No Trace practices, bully breed advocacy, and efforts to end BSL (breed-specific legislation). Most recently, they have invited their kitties to join us on shorter hikes! You can find them on Instagram @adventurepittieand3kitties.

JOANNA LEE lives in Colorado with her two dogs, Kane and Nyx. They love the outdoors and are avid hikers year-round. You can find them on all types of hikes, from Colorado's highest peaks to its beautiful alpine lakes and snow-covered forests. You can follow their adventures on Instagram @co_mountainpack.

AMBER PITCHER lives in upstate New York with her dog, Ariel. She has given her the courage to pursue adventure, and together they have climbed hundreds of mountains, traveled the country, and discovered a love for paddleboarding. During the week, she works as a veterinary technician, but on weekends you can find them exploring their home in the Adirondack and Catskill Mountains. She and Ariel share their lives with Amber's husband, Matt, and their two cats, Ollie and Floki.

DAWN MELLON, a professional dog trainer, started training and competing in dog sports as a kid thirty-five years ago and has over fifteen years of experience as a veterinary technician. She has instructed, trained, titled, and certified dogs in agility, obedience, rally, tracking, conformation, nosework, Frisbee, search and rescue, therapy, and service dogs. She hiked almost 1,500 miles of the PCT in 2018 with her border collie, Emily. When she's not training dogs, her hobbies include hiking, backpacking, trail running, mountaineering, and rock climbing. She is the owner and trainer at www.themissingleash.com and owner and operator of www.thehikerpup.com. You can find them on Facebook and Instagram @ thehikerpup.

JANE PATTEN has spent the last twenty years living in eastern Washington and loves calling Spokane her home. There's no shortage of recreation east of the Cascades, where she spends her free time exploring trails with her rescue pup, Moose.

KATHERINE TAYLOR hikes in the Los Angeles area with her little dog, Robin, and husband, Addison. She tests out all the cool dog gear she can get her hands on. Follow their adventures on Instagram @robinventures and read all the gear reviews on robinventures .wordpress.com.

RORY RILEY TOPPING is an attorney and legal analyst for Spectrum News Networks. In her spare time, she and her husband, Richard, enjoy hiking the Blue Ridge Mountains and training their two rescued Dobermans, Boston and Griffin. You can follow their adventures on Instagram @dobiesisters.

JESSICA WILLIAMS has been camping and hiking with her dogs for over fifteen years and is author of the award-winning blog https://youdidwhatwithyourwiener.com. There she shares her tips and experience with others to help them get active with their dogs in the outdoors. You can follow their adventures on Instagram at @youdidwhatwithyourwiener.

HANNAH ZULUETA resides in San Diego. She has two Boston terriers and has been organizing pack walks for the past three years. You can find her on her blog https:// maggielovesorbit.com or on Instagram @maggielovesorbit.com.

PHOTO CREDITS

Morgan Williams & Griffey @griffeyflood

Stephanie Alexander & Arrietty and Frankie @travelingspaghettis

Luz Lopez & Benz @benztheshep

Laura McIntyre & Roman @roman.around.scotland

Sachi Abe & Clementine @darling_clem

Stephanie Clemens & Storm and Frankie @pupfrankie

Alyssa Salava & Zigzag @alyssasalava

Hannah Ellison & Colonel @colonels_corner

Kimmi Day & Key @kimmi.ambles

Staci Kates & Merci @merciandme

Katelyn Ward & Meru and Cooper @meru.the.heeler

Nena Damson & Rainier and Baker @the_mountain_dogs

Laurin Smith & Ranger @la_la_laurin

Deb Balcanoff & Jake @lechdb1

Alison Whipple @ Apollo @apollothefabulous

Allison Strange & Sookie @sookiesupernova

Abigail Baines & Jasper @mylifewithjasper

Anna Peterson & Yuki @adventure.yuki

Ellen Rempel & Pico @wonderpico

Michal Forys & Arath and Luna @arath.and.luna

Jamie Bush & Isadora, Gianni, and Emma

Jura Craven & Tala @tala_the_nubianhound

INDEX

ABOUT THE AUTHOR

JEN SOTOLONGO lives in Oregon with her dog, Sitka, a rescued red heeler mix. They're up for just about any outdoor activity, as long as they can do it together. More often than not, they're on a trail run in the mountains. Jen is the author of the blog longhaultrekkers .com, a source for adventure dog parents to get outdoors and travel with their dogs. You can follow Jen and Sitka on Instagram @longhaultrekkers.